Everyday Life of the Aztecs

Frontispiece: Reconstruction of the centre of Tenochtitlán

Everyday Life of
THE AZTECS

WARWICK BRAY

Drawings by Eva Wilson

DORSET PRESS
New York

To my wife

First published by B.T. Batsford 1968

This edition published by Dorset Press,
a division of Marboro Books Corporation,
by arrangement with B.T. Batsford Ltd.
1987 Dorset Press

ISBN 0-88029-143-5

Printed in the United States of America
M 9 8 7 6 5 4 3

CONTENTS

ACKNOWLEDGMENT

For help during the preparation of this work the Author is grateful to the staff of Sheffield University Library for obtaining rare books, to Mr Peter Kemmis Betty and Miss Audrey Geber of B. T. Batsford Ltd for their helpfulness and patience with a most dilatory author, and to Mrs Eva Wilson whose drawings have brought the Aztecs to life again in a way which words alone could never have done.

The Author and Publishers wish to thank the following for permission to reproduce the illustrations appearing in this book: The Instituto Nacional de Antropología e Historia, Mexico City for frontispiece, figs. 40, 41, 44, 53, 71, 87; Mrs J. March-Penney for figs. 5 and 56; The Trustees of the British Museum for figs. 8, 13, 60, 61, 64, 85, 89, 94; Cambridge University Museum of Archaeology and Ethnology for figs. 14, 67; Liverpool City Museum for figs. 28 and 82; Radio Times Hulton Picture Library for fig. 81; Museum of the American Indian, New York for fig. 59; Württemburgischen Landesmuseum, Stuttgart for fig. 75; Museum für Völkerkunde, Vienna for fig. 92; Stanford University Press, publishers of *The Ancient Maya* (Third Edition) by S. G. Morley, revised by G. W. Brainerd, 1946, 1947, 1956 for fig. 79; Instituto Nacional de Antropología e Historia, Mexico, publishers of I. Marquina's *El Templo Mayor de Mexico* 1960 for figs. 31 and 38 and *Arquitectura Prehispánica* 1951 for fig. 90; Thames and Hudson, publishers of M. Coe's *Mexico* 1962 for fig. 80; Bodleian Library Oxford for figs. 4, 18, 19, MS. Arch. Selden A.1.

Acknowledgment is also due to the publishers for permission to quote from the following books: Editorial Porrua, Mexico, *Historia de la Literatura Náhuatl* by A. M. Garibay, 1953–54; Beacon Press, *The Broken Spears* edited by M. León-Portilla, 1962; University of Oklahoma Press, *Aztec Thought and Culture* by M. León-Portilla, 1959; Thames & Hudson Ltd, *Mexico* by M. Coe, 1962; J. M. Dent & Sons Ltd, *Lords of New Spain* by Alonso de Zorita (edited by B. Keen), 1965; Weidenfeld & Nicolson Ltd, *The Daily Life of the Aztecs* by J. Soustelle, 1961; University of Utah and Santa Fé School of American Research, *Codex Florentino* by Fray Bernardino de Sahagún, translated by A. J. O. Anderson and C. E. Dibble, 1950–59; University of California, Berkeley, *Ibero-Americana*; Hutchinson Publishing Group, *The Spanish Seaborne Empire* by J. H. Parry, 1966; Secretaria de Educación Pública, Mexico, *La Religión de los Aztecas* by A. Caso, 1945.

THE ILLUSTRATIONS

7

PREFACE

In 1519 Hernando Cortés and a small Spanish army landed on the east coast of Mexico. From that moment the Aztecs became a part of European history, and as Europeans (in the cultural rather than the geographical sense of the word) our reaction to Mexican civilization is usually not very different from that of a sixteenth-century Spaniard. We share Cortés' amazement at the richness of a civilization which lacked the arch, the wheel, iron tools, alphabetic writing, and so many of the things which we take for granted, and—like him—we are repelled by Mexican religion with its idolatry and human sacrifices.

Yet the things which seemed so strange and exotic to the Spaniards were to the Indians just a part of normal everyday life. From the Mexican point of view it was the Spaniards who were odd, with their pale complexions and outlandish clothes, their horses and gunpowder, uncouth manners, and lack of reverence for the gods who controlled the Aztec universe.

This book is an attempt to reconstruct Mexican life on the eve of the Conquest, using both archaeological evidence and early documentary sources. I have drawn on the writings of men who took part in the Conquest and who saw with their own eyes the city of Tenochtitlán before its destruction. The letters which Cortés wrote to the Emperor Charles V during the years 1519–26 include many descriptions of Aztec life, and can be supplemented from the eyewitness accounts left by four of his companions: Bernal Díaz del Castillo, Andres de Tapia, Francisco de Aguilar, and an anonymous soldier who describes himself simply as 'a gentleman attached to Señor Fernando Cortés'.

After the soldiers came the churchmen, many of them learned and sympathetic people who strove to understand the customs of the Indians among whom they worked. The first group of Franciscan friars reached Mexico only three years after the Conquest, and among their number was Toribio de Benavente, nicknamed

9

Motolinía (the Poor One), whose *Memoriales* and *History of the Indians of New Spain* are filled with his own observations of Indian life.

The greatest figure in Aztec studies is another Franciscan, Bernardino de Sahagún, who came to Mexico in 1529 and spent most of his life there. His *General History of the Things of New Spain* was originally written in Nahuatl, the language of the Aztecs, and was compiled, often verbatim, from information supplied by natives who had experienced the things they described, and who had learned many historical and religious texts by heart as part of their education in the traditional Mexican schools. Under the title *Florentine Codex* Arthur J. O. Anderson and Charles E. Dibble have prepared an English edition which exactly captures the flavour of Aztec speech with all its circumlocutions and repetitions. Quotations attributed to Sahagún without any further acknowledgment are taken from the Anderson-Dibble text.

In his *Brief and Summary Account of the Lords of New Spain* the Spanish administrator, Alonso de Zorita, has left one of the best sixteenth-century descriptions of the Aztec clan system and land tenure, and from the same period we have historical works written by Spaniards, like Diego Durán, and by hispanicized Indians of whom the most important are Tezozomoc and Ixtlilxochitl.

Another valuable source of information is a group of manuscripts (or *codices*) in Aztec picture writing. Although most examples are of post-Conquest date they incorporate a lot of pre-Spanish material. One of them, the *Codex Mendoza*, contains a copy of Montezuma's Tribute List and a treatise on the education of children. Others include scenes of everyday life as well as pictures of household articles, clothes, gods, and calendrical signs.

Of more recent literature I owe a special debt to three books: *The Aztecs, People of the Sun* by Alfonso Caso, *Aztec Thought and Culture* by M. León-Portilla, and *The Daily Life of the Aztecs* by Jacques Soustelle. The works of Olmos, Sahagún, and Zorita incorporate many songs and speeches taken from Mexican oral literature, but no study of that subject would be complete without reference to A. M. Garibay's *Historia de la Literatura Náhuatl* with its many translations from original Nahuatl texts.

In the Romanization of Mexican names I have tried to follow the most common usage, even though this is not always the most correct one. The traditional rendering *Montezuma* for example, has been preferred to the more accurate *Moctezuma* or *Motecuhzoma*. The pronunciation of Nahuatl is not as difficult as it appears: *x* has the sound of English *sh*; *z* is more like the English *s*; *hu* before a vowel is pronounced like *w*. All vowels (including *e* when it occurs at the end of a word) are pronounced as in modern Spanish or Italian.

Setting and History

Mexico is a land of contrasts. Within its boundaries are vast deserts, mountain peaks on which the snow never melts, and lush tropical forests (the 'Hot Lands') which stretch in a narrow belt along the coastal plain all the way from the south-eastern United States to the Yucatan peninsula. Climate depends more on altitude than on latitude, and as the rainfall and temperature change so too do the crops, agricultural methods, harvest times, animal life, and raw materials.

Above all, Mexico is a land of mountains. The country is shaped like a cornucopia with its wider end opening to the north. Most of its territory lies above 3,000 feet, and the spine of the country is in the form of a Y made up of mountain chains which follow the outline of the coasts, although their crests lie between 100 and 200 miles from the sea. The western arm of the Y is the higher of the two ranges, and between it and the eastern arm stretches a plateau of grassland and mesquite which in its more barren parts comes near to true desert. Farming was impossible in this arid zone, and it remained the homeland of barbarian peoples who lived by hunting and collecting wild plants. The Aztec way of life, based on agriculture and urbanism, could not flourish in the plateau region, and no attempt was made to incorporate this useless land into the Aztec empire.

Some 300 miles north of Mexico City (which under the name of Tenochtitlán was also the Aztec capital) the two cordilleras converge to form the Central Highlands, a country broken up by mountain ranges into a number of inland valleys, each of which is separated from the others and, because of the variation in altitude, has an environment peculiar to itself.

The greatest of these valleys, the homeland of the Aztecs

and—for a while, at least—the limit of their political ambitions, is the Valley of Mexico. It lies towards the southern edge of the Central Highlands at a height of about a mile and a half above sea level. Strictly speaking, it is not a valley at all but an intramontane basin with no natural outlet. In shape it is like a figure 8, measuring roughly 75 miles from north to south by 40 miles across, and enclosing an area of about 3,000 square miles. To the south-east it is overlooked by the snow-capped peaks of the volcanoes Popocatépetl (Smoking Mountain) and Iztaccíhuatl (White Lady), and the entire valley is rimmed by mountains which, although not a barrier to the movement of peoples, do serve to mark off the Aztec heartland from the rest of the country (1).

Nowadays it is a dry and treeless land, perpetually dusty. For most of the year the landscape is a patchwork of browns and earth colours, turning green only during the spring months when the crops are growing. The mountain crests were never inhabited or cultivated, but in Aztec times the higher slopes still bore forests of pine, spruce, cedar and oak, while the lower hillsides with their fertile soil were intensively farmed. Today the forests have gone. The process of deforestation had begun long before the Spaniards arrived, for each successive Indian civilization had cut down trees to provide building-timber, firewood, and fuel for the lime-burners who manu-factured plaster for the walls of innumerable temples and palaces. The Spaniards wrought even greater destruction than the Indians. The forest was cleared faster than it could re-generate, and with the disappearance of the tree cover and the introduction of sheep and goats from Europe came the inevitable erosion.

More important than the rivers (which were uncontrollable torrents during the wet summer months and dry gullies in winter) was the lake which occupied the central part of the Valley. Post-Conquest drainage has reduced the lake to a fraction of its former size, but in the Aztec period it was vital to the economy of the Valley, providing fish and wildfowl, fresh water for drinking and irrigation, and reeds used for thatching, basketry and mat-making. Bulky goods could easily be trans-ported by canoe from one lakeside town to another, and the city of Tenochtitlán was built over the water, with its houses standing on piles or on islands separated by canals.

The lake was only 9–12 feet deep and was divided into five units, each of which had its own name, although all five formed part of the same system(1). The three northern lakes were salty because the minerals brought down by the streams were unable to flush away through any natural outlet, but lakes Chalco and Xochimilco, which were continuously replenished by melting snow and by springs of sweet water, remained fresh all the year round.

The Valley of Mexico had no gold or cotton of its own, but was otherwise well provided with the necessities of life. Salt, building-stone, timber, and obsidian for tool-making could all be obtained locally, and the climate was pleasant, with enough rain in the months from June to September to guarantee an adequate maize harvest in a normal year. At the time of the Conquest the Valley supported between one and three million people and contained more than 20 towns, not to mention villages and smaller settlements.

In the middle of the sixteenth century the Aztecs initiated a policy of expansion, adding new lands to their domain and meeting conditions very different from those of the Valley. To the south, in the modern states of Morelos and Puebla, is a region of warm and humid valleys drained by the Rio Balsas and its tributaries. Here, between 3,000 and 6,000 feet above sea level, the Indians were able to grow cotton and semi-tropical fruits, especially where irrigation could ensure a constant water supply. Still further south lie the hills of Oaxaca, rich in the copper and gold which the Valley of Mexico lacked.

The 'Hot Lands' of the Gulf Coast are different again. Here the climate is torrid all the year round, in contrast with the Valley where there is frost on winter nights, and even an occasional fall of snow. The high summer rainfall, more than twice that of the highlands, encourages a thick growth of forest, and the highland type of agriculture is replaced by shifting cultivation. From this region the Aztecs obtained rubber, cocoa, jaguar skins, and the feathers of tropical birds.

Mexico before the Aztecs

The roots of Aztec civilization reach deep into the past. During the thousand years before the birth of Christ a distinctively Mexican pattern of life was emerging, and by the start of the

13

Christian era many elements of Aztec culture had already made their appearance. The more advanced tribes were by this time constructing great religious centres in which the most important buildings were temples standing on pyramid-shaped platforms. Their priests knew how to write in hieroglyphic symbols, and their astronomers had begun to use the 52-year calendric cycle which was one of the bases of Aztec religious thought. At this early date there is already evidence for the ritual ball-game which was played by most of the Mexican nations until the Spanish Conquest.

From roughly A.D. 300–600 the central part of the country was dominated by the city of Teotihuacán, only 30 miles away from the site which was to become the Aztec capital. By any standards Teotihuacán was a great city. It covered more than seven square miles, and at its centre was an area of temple-platforms and palaces over which rose the gigantic pyramids of the Sun and Moon. Many of the buildings were adorned with carvings or frescoes in which can be recognized deities who were still worshipped in Aztec times: Tlaloc (the Rain God), Quetzalcoatl (the Plumed Serpent)(70), Chalchihuit-licue (the Water Goddess), Xipe Totec (Our Lord the Flayed One) and many others.

In about 600 Teotihuacán was overthrown, and by the Aztec period even the name of its builders had been forgotten, although the city figures in legends as a centre of civilization and learning, and as the place where the gods assembled to create the sun. Its location was still remembered, however, and Montezuma, last of the Aztec rulers, made several pilgrimages to its ruins.

The other people who make frequent appearances in Aztec mythology and history are the Toltecs whose capital was at Tollan, the present-day Tula. In the legends, Tollan is a sort of never-never land where there were palaces of gold and turquoise, where the ears of maize were as big as milling stones and the amaranth plants so tall that men climbed up them. Guided by the god Quetzalcoatl, the Toltecs discovered the skills of medicine and astronomy, were the first to use the calendar, and lived a life of ease, listening to the birds, composing music, and working gold and precious stones.

The truth is more prosaic. The Toltecs were a very real people who held sway over most of central Mexico from the tenth to

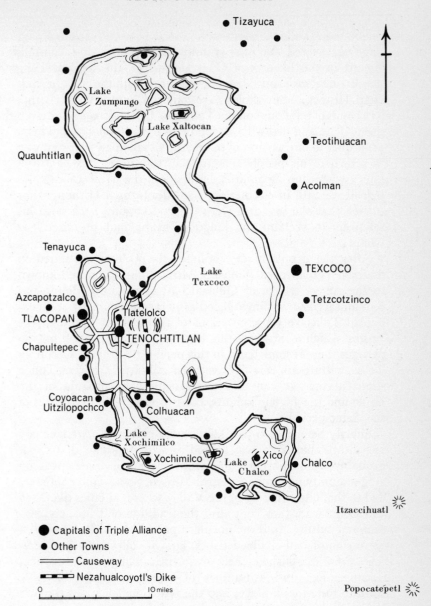

Tizayuca

Lake
Zumpango

Lake Xaltocan

Quauhtitlan

Teotihuacan

Acolman

Tenayuca

Lake
Texcoco

TEXCOCO

Azcapotzalco

Tetzcotzinco

TLACOPAN

Tlatelolco

Chapultepec

TENOCHTITLAN

Coyoacan
Uitzilopochco

Colhuacan

Lake
Xochimilco

Xochimilco

Lake
Chalco

Xico

Chalco

Itzaccihuatl

● Capitals of Triple Alliance
● Other Towns
═══ Causeway
▄▬▄ Nezahualcoyotl's Dike

0   10 miles

Popocatepetl

1 The Valley of Mexico in Aztec times

the twelfth centuries A.D. Their second ruler, Topíltzin, was born in about 935 and moved his capital to Tula where archaeologists have discovered temple-pyramids, ball-courts, and columns carved in the likeness of Quetzalcoatl. In the legends King Topíltzin seems to have become identified with the god Quetzalcoatl. History and mythology are confused, but the story tells that as a result of religious conflict Topíltzin-Quetzalcoatl was driven out of Tula and fled with his followers to the Gulf Coast. There, according to one version of the myth, he sailed away, promising to return to his people sometime in the future. Six centuries later, when the Spaniards landed on the Gulf Coast, this legend was still in circulation, and Montezuma II thought for a time that the invaders were the god coming back with his followers to reclaim the kingdom as he had promised (*see* Chapter 10).

After the expulsion of Topíltzin the Toltecs continued to flourish. Tezcatlipoca (Smoking Mirror)(78), a god well known to the Aztecs, replaced Quetzalcoatl as the chief deity, and human sacrifice was introduced as part of his cult. At archaeological Tula are representations of the skull rack and of the vessels which contained the hearts of sacrificed victims, so perhaps there is some truth in this part of the legend. Certainly Toltec culture appears to have been militaristic, and in Toltec stone-carving we can already recognize the insignia of the Eagle and the Jaguar knights, the two great military orders of the Aztec period.

Shortly before 1200 the Toltec state collapsed. Archaeology has shown that Tula was sacked and its buildings destroyed, probably by barbarian tribes from the north. There was no longer a unifying force in central Mexico. Some Toltec refugees fled to the southern part of the Valley where, at cities like Xico and Colhuacán, they kept alive the tradition of Toltec civilization and culture. Into the northern part of the Valley moved a succession of half-civilized tribes, known collectively as *Chichimecs*, who established their own little states at Tenayuca, Azcapotzalco, and a number of other cities. Gradually a cultural fusion took place, and the newcomers learned the arts of civilization from the descendants of the Toltecs. In a sense, therefore, we can trace a continuity from the Toltecs to their Chichimec successors. The intruders, for their part, claimed that by virtue of conquest and possession they were the rightful

2 The early history of the Aztecs. The Mexicans leave their island home, cross the lake by canoe in the year One Flint, 1168, and eventually arrive at a cave in a hillside where they discover a miraculous speaking idol of Huitzilopochtli
(Codex Boturini, c. 1540)

heirs of the Toltecs, and several Chichimec dynasties tried to give substance to this claim by marrying into noble Toltec families.

The growth of the Aztec state

The last of the barbarian tribes to enter the Valley was the Nahuatl-speaking group which we know as the Aztecs, although they referred to themselves as the *Mexica* or as the *Tenochca*. The name Mexico was not used for the country as a whole until after the Spanish Conquest, and in the original sense of the word the 'Mexicans' are simply the 'Aztecs', the people whose capital city was Mexico-Tenochtitlán.

The early history of these people is obscure, and their first appearance on the historical scene is no earlier than the thirteenth century when they infiltrated the Valley of Mexico. Their original homeland has yet to be located, but according to their own records and legends they left it in 1168 and spent about a century wandering all over the country before settling down on the shores of Lake Texcoco (2). The figure 1168 must not be taken too seriously, but—mythological or not—it is one of the dates suggested in the annals for the abandonment of Tula and the break-up of the Toltec empire. By implication, then, the travels of the Aztecs formed part of the movement of barbarian tribes which followed the collapse of the old order and led to the Chichimec incursions into the Valley of Mexico.

Aztec history falls naturally into three phases: a period of wandering ended by the founding of Tenochtitlán, a period during which the Aztecs consolidated their position in the Valley of Mexico, and finally a period of expansion and conquest which was brought to an end when the Aztecs were themselves conquered by the Spaniards in 1521.

1 The Period of Wandering, 1168–1325

For this period the only documentation is in the form of legends, often contradictory and invariably written down long after the happenings which they claim to describe had taken place.

In one version of the story the Aztecs originally came from Aztlán, an island in the middle of a lake. They crossed in their canoes to the shore, and there, in a cave in the hillside, discovered the idol of Huitzilopochtli which was to lead them on their travels (2). From this place they set out, accompanied by a number of other tribes which were the ancestors of those who set up little kingdoms in the Valley of Mexico during the Chichimec interlude. The group broke up, the other tribes moving off to conquer territory where they could set up their own states, and the Aztecs continued alone, taking the advice of their god and worshipping him at each stopping-place. During this migration they changed their name to *Mexica*. Eventually they came to the Valley of Mexico where they found the best land already occupied.

The impression left by these legends, although untrustworthy in detail, is probably not far from the truth. The Aztecs figure as a migratory tribe, perhaps only a few thousand strong, and just one among the several groups of Chichimecs set into motion by the Toltec collapse. At best, the Mexica-Aztec were only half civilized. They practised agriculture of a rather impermanent kind, wore clothes of maguey fibre cloth, and (though this is doubtful at such an early date) their priests may have been literate. They must be classed among those Chichimec tribes which had lived on the fringe of civilization long enough to have acquired farming and a few useful arts from their more advanced neighbours, as opposed to the 'Teochichi-meca', the 'extreme' Chichimecs of Mexican annals, who remained primitive hunters.

The Aztecs entered the Valley from the north-west, by way of Tula and Zumpango, only to find that there was nowhere for them to live. For a while they gained a precarious living, squatting on other people's land and being continually moved on. From about 1250 to 1298 they were the vassals of Azcapot-zalco, the capital of the Tepanec kingdom. Then they lived under the overlordship of Colhuacán until in 1323 they were foolish enough to sacrifice a Colhua princess on the altar of Huitzilopochtli. Once more the Aztecs were driven out, and the tribe took refuge in the swamps of Lake Texcoco.

Here the outcasts lived a miserable and savage existence on a group of uninhabited islands surrounded by marshes, left in peace only because the other nations thought they were not worth the trouble of exterminating and because the territory they had chosen was a sort of no man's land between the borders of Azcapotzalco to the north, Texcoco to the east, and Col-huacán in the south. None of these powers was willing to risk war with the others for the possession of a few useless islands.

It was in this inhospitable environment that the Aztecs founded their city in the year *Ome Acatl*, Two-Reed (variously given as 1325, 1344, or 1345). They called the site Tenochtitlán, Place of the Prickly Pear Cactus.

2 Consolidation in the Valley of Mexico, 1325–1440

This was a period of confusion when the new states in the Valley had not yet achieved a balance of power. These petty kingdoms, consisting sometimes of only one city and rarely of more than three or four important towns, squabbled among themselves as enthusiastically as the city states of Classical Greece or Renaissance Italy, and for much the same reasons—to extend political influence, to squeeze even heavier taxes from tributary towns, or to gain a little bit more territory here or there. Although these wars and disagreements bulk large in the histories, it is worthwhile recalling the small scale of the operations. As Vaillant has pointed out, tourists can travel round the entire theatre of war by car in a single day.

Tenochtitlán began as a collection of reed huts surrounding the temple of Huitzilopochtli on one muddy island. Legends maintain that the sister town of Tlatelolco was founded at roughly the same time on a similar island only a mile to the north (the name means Place of the Mounds), but recent excavations have shown that an earlier settlement existed on the site. Whatever the previous history of Tlatelolco, it soon became an Aztec town and, with Tenochtitlán, came under the yoke of the Tepanec kingdom of Azcapotzalco, at this time entering a period of expansion under the rule of Tezozomoc. The Mexica-Aztec were forced to pay tribute and to fight as mercenaries in the wars of their overlord.

The clusters of huts were gradually transformed into stone-built towns, and by the middle of the fourteenth century both Tenochtitlán and Tlatelolco were large enough to petition the mainland tribes to provide them with chiefs. Tenochtitlán got its first real monarch in the person of Acamapichtli (1367-87), a prince of the dynasty of Colhuacán, and Tlatelolco was allotted to a son of Tezozomoc.

Throughout the reign of Huitzilihuitl, the second ruler of Tenochtitlán who reigned from 1397 to 1415, the Aztecs remained under the suzerainty of Azcapotzalco which had by now swallowed up its only serious rival, the state of Texcoco on the eastern shore of the lake, and had emerged as the most powerful kingdom of the Valley. But Tepanec power was not to last. In 1426 the aged Tezozomoc died and was succeeded on the throne of Azcapotzalco by Maxtla, a bitter enemy of Tenochtitlán. One of his first actions was to arrange the murder of the lord of Tlatelolco, and then, in 1426, of Chimalpopoca, the third ruler of Tenochtitlán. Chimalpopoca was succeeded by Itzcoatl (1427-40) who organized a grand alliance with the aim of breaking the grip of Azcapotzalco. He was joined by the lakeside towns of Tlatelolco and Tlacopan, and by the defeated Texcocans under Nezahualcoyotl, their ruler-in-exile. The allies requested help from Tlaxcala and Uexotzinco, two states outside the Valley altogether, and the combined forces mounted an operation which regained Texcoco for its legitimate heir and captured the principal Tepanec cities. By 1428, the power of Azcapotzalco was broken.

This victory was the turning point in Aztec history. The allies found themselves the inheritors of the Tepanec empire—if such a grand word can be used for so small a territory—and the gains were shared out between them. The Texcocans recovered their city and its tributary towns, and from then on controlled the eastern shore of the lake; Tlacopan received land on the western side; the Aztecs gained their first foothold on the mainland when they took over some of the Nahuatl-speaking areas to the north and south. The victors were now in a position to dictate terms to the other states of the Valley, and the situation was formalized in the Triple Alliance, a treaty between Tenochtitlán, Texcoco and Tlacopan, which provided for mutual defence and a sharing out of the spoils of future conquests—two shares each for Texcoco and Tenochtitlán (which between them provided most of the warriors) and one share for Tlacopan (which was chiefly responsible for transport and provisions). This Triple Alliance dominated Mexican politics for the next century. Nominally at least, the rulers of Texcoco and Tenochtitlán were joint heads of what is often called the 'Aztec Empire', and this fiction was maintained long after Tenochtitlán had become the dominant partner. It was not until the reign of Montezuma II, immediately before the Spanish Conquest, that Texcoco lost its position and became a client state.

The victory had its psychological as well as its political effects. At one stroke Tenochtitlán was transformed from a tributary island kingdom into a major power which could demand tribute from others and which had acquired interests on the mainland. The Aztecs had learned that aggression pays, and the discovery changed the entire basis of their society. During their early wanderings they had been a nation of soldier-peasants organized into a fairly democratic society with little of the hierarchical class structure so evident in later years. But increased power and responsibility required a different kind of leadership. The warrior caste grew in influence and prestige at the expense of the farmers. Control of everyday affairs passed increasingly into the hands of the nobility and the professional administrators, while the people as a whole developed a new confidence, a feeling of superiority over all other nationalities.

This attitude was deliberately fostered by Itzcoatl and his chief minister, Tlacaelel. It was at this time that the old history books were burned because they laid too much emphasis on the barbarian origins of the Aztecs. Itzcoatl made similar attempts to destroy the records of the older-established kingdoms because these either left out the Aztecs as unworthy of notice or else made frank references to their former condition.

The Mexicans now felt themselves to be a chosen people whose self-appointed mission was to conquer in the name of Huitzilo-pochtli.

The smaller kingdoms of the Valley were soon disposed of, and the supremacy of the Triple Alliance was assured when Chalco and Xochimilco capitulated. The whole of the Valley of Mexico was now under the control of the Allies. Further conquests could only be made outside this closed little world, but after one campaign, in which he subdued part of Morelos, Itzcoatl died.

3 Expansion and Conquest, 1440–1521

Montezuma I (1440–68) continued the aggressive policy of his predecessor. He captured territory from the Mixtecs in the south-west, and his armies swept through the eastern lands until they reached the Gulf Coast in the Huasteca and Vera Cruz. For the first time, a highland state was able to exact tribute from the Hot Lands. Exotic products (chocolate, rubber, cotton, tropical fruits, and rare plumage) which had once been novelties, reached Tenochtitlán in ever-increasing quantities, altering the habits of the aristocracy and creating new demands which could be satisfied only by further con-quests. Captives taken during the fighting were sacrificed to Huitzilopochtli, and these prisoners became as essential to Mexican religion as the new raw materials did to the economy.

Meanwhile Tenochtitlán was growing from a state capital into an imperial city, and at the same time its principal ally, Texcoco, was entering its golden age under the rule of Neza-hualcoyotl. Of the two cities, Tenochtitlán was the more powerful but Texcoco became the intellectual and artistic centre of the Valley. The purest and most elegant form of Nahuatl was spoken there, and Nezahualcoyotl himself was an orator whose poems and speeches were remembered for centuries after his death. He drew up a legal code, interested himself in philosophy, religion, and astronomy, and invited the finest craftsmen to his court where a commission awarded prizes for outstanding achievement. Nezahualcoyotl must have been a skilful diplomatist as well, for he somehow managed to remain at peace with his domineering neighbours.

Under Axayácatl (1469–81) the Mexicans made further conquests, and during his reign Tlatelolco lost its independence.

Tenochtitlán and Tlatelolco, the two original Aztec foundations, had grown in importance together, but the commercial reputation of Tlatelolco, which had the greatest market in the land, so aroused the envy of the Tenochcas that in 1473 they seized upon the insulting behaviour of a few Tlatelolcan women as a pretext for invasion. Tlatelolco was defeated, its chief killed and replaced by a Tenochcan military governor, and the city council deprived of its right to a voice in Aztec policy formation.

Tizoc, a brother of Axayácatl, was a weak ruler who died after only six years on the throne, poisoned, it is said, by the military chiefs who wanted to replace him by a more warlike leader. They found the right man in Ahuítzotl, who ruled from 1486 to 1502. Under his leadership, the armies of the Triple Alliance captured further territory from the Mixtecs and Huastecs, and broke through to the Pacific coast where they established Aztec supremacy as far south as the present-day border with Guatemala.

The last of the pre-Conquest rulers was Montezuma II, a son of Axayácatl. In the final years of the Empire he added new lands round the border of the Mixteca, and one of his last actions was to break up the Triple Alliance. Tlacopan had long ago ceased to count for anything, and the alliance was effectively a partnership between Texcoco and Tenochtitlán. Inevitably there was rivalry between the two cities, but during the reign of Nezahualcoyotl and his successor, the equally able Nezahualpilli, a precarious peace was maintained. When Nezahualpilli died in 1516, the Tenochcas appointed their own candidate to the throne against the wishes of the Texcocan council. The Texcocans rose in rebellion, and the alliance was broken.

It was this Empire, still expanding its territory, and at the height of its glory when Cortés began his invasion in 1519, which was to be so unexpectedly overturned.

The Empire in 1519

On the eve of the Conquest the Empire stretched from the Atlantic to the Pacific coasts, northwards as far as the desert where settled life was impossible, and southwards into the hills of Oaxaca. In addition the Mexicans controlled a trade route

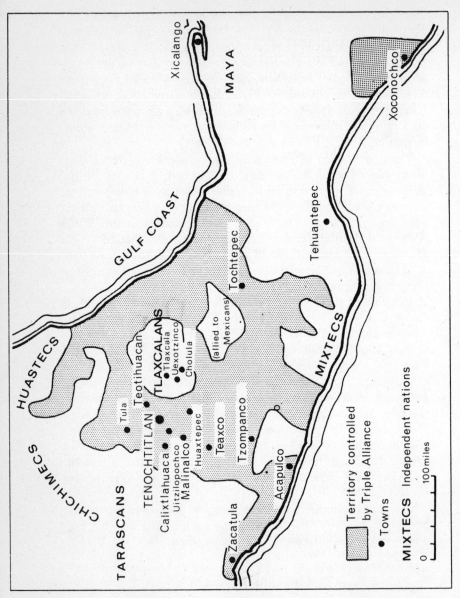

Xicalango

MAYA

Xoconochco

GULF COAST

Tehuantepec

Tochtepec

(allied to Mexicans)

HUASTECS

TLAXCALANS
Teotihuacan
Tlaxcala
Uexotzinco
Cholula

MIXTECS

TARASCANS

CHICHIMECS

Tula

TENOCHTITLAN
Calixtlahuaca
Uitzilopochco
Malinalco
Huaxtepec
Teaxco
Tzompanco

Zacatula

Acapulco

Territory controlled
by Triple Alliance

● Towns

MIXTECS Independent nations

100 miles

0

3 Mexico on the eve of the Spanish Conquest

leading further south along the Pacific coast to end near the Guatemalan border in the province of Xoconochco, which formed an isolated part of the Empire (3). Within the borders of the Empire were 489 tributary towns (divided for administrative convenience into 38 provinces), and some 15 million people, most of whom were not Aztecs.

Even in the Valley of Mexico the Aztecs were only one of several nationalities. The various groups which made their way into the Valley after the Toltec collapse are best described as tribes, and at the time of the Conquest, when the Aztecs—or more accurately the Triple Alliance—ruled over the whole area, the old tribal groups still recognized themselves as entities. The tributary or allied peoples kept careful note of their boundaries, and many of their documents deal with land records. Nezahualcoyotl, the ruler of Texcoco, built walls and placed markers to indicate the frontiers of his domain, and in his capital there were separate quarters for Mexicans, Culhuas, and Tepanecs.

These ethnic distinctions were partly masked by a cultural unity in which the Nahuatl language, spoken by all the Valley peoples except the Otomí, was an important factor. The tribes had lived side by side for many generations and, with certain local variations, shared in a common economic, religious, and political tradition which was largely an inheritance from the Toltecs. Even so, a man's first loyalty was to his own tribe, and the subject peoples did not consider themselves Aztecs.

Outside the confines of the Valley, the Aztecs encountered other peoples who differed among themselves in language, customs, dress, religion, and way of life. The hill tribes around the perimeter of the Valley had a culture similar to that of the Aztecs and might even speak Nahuatl, but differences became more marked the further one travelled from the Valley of Mexico. In the south-west lived the Mixtecs and the Zapotecs, with their own languages and with cultural traditions more ancient than that of the Aztecs. The Hot Lands were inhabited by the civilized and elegant Totonacs, whose northern neighbours, the Huastecs, spoke a Maya dialect. Although Nahuatl became the lingua franca of the Empire, more than 20 distinct languages were spoken within its frontiers.

The Aztecs were not interested in imposing their own form

of civilization on the conquered nations. Although they did insist that their own god, Huitzilopochtli, should be worshipped alongside the local deities, there was no attempt to make the subjects abandon their own religion. The Allies, unlike the Spaniards, did not pretend that their mission was to bring light to the heathen, nor did they justify their conquests by claiming that everything was for the benefit of the conquered people. As long as the cities of the Triple Alliance received tribute and obedience they were satisfied (4). Tax-gatherers were sent to the provincial capitals, Aztec governors were installed, and if necessary military garrisons were stationed in potential trouble spots. Occasional large-scale transfers of population are reported in the histories, but usually the life of the region went on as before. Language and local customs were not interfered with, nor was the political structure altered. Strictly speaking, the 'Aztec Empire' was not an empire at all. The basic unit of Mexican politics was the city state, and although Tenochtitlán was able to exact tribute from many other cities by force of arms the Aztecs never consolidated their conquests into a politically unified empire. It was fear rather than loyalty which kept the subject provinces faithful to Tenochtitlán, as they showed at the time of the Conquest when many of them threw in their lot with the Spaniards.

Certain nations resisted the power of the Alliance and were still independent when the Spaniards arrived. Along the northern frontiers of the Empire lived the nomadic Chichimecs, a hardy race of hunters and bowmen whom the Aztecs romanticized as a nation of 'noble savages'—a common enough myth among city-dwellers who have never experienced the life they so admire!

More important were two powerful and civilized nations who were never subdued. To the west lived the Tarascans. The Aztec ruler, Axayácatl, had tried to conquer them, but he was defeated in battle and the attempt was not repeated. Nearer at hand lay Tlaxcala, a state which had fought alongside Tenochtitlán in the revolt against Azcapotzalco, but which soon became a bitter enemy. The conquests of Axayácatl had left Tlaxcala completely encircled by Mexican territory. There was constant war between the two states, and it is possible that the Aztecs deliberately refrained from crushing Tlaxcala because they found the war a useful source of

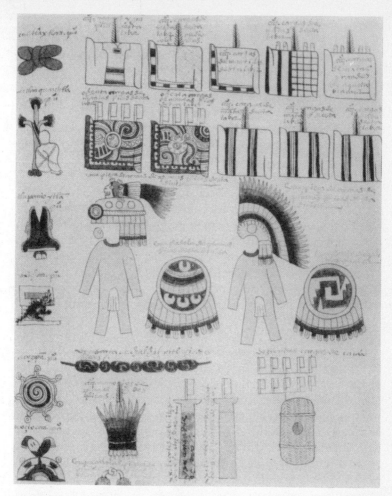

4 A page from Montezuma's Tribute List (Codex Mendoza). Down the left-hand edge are glyphs for six tributary towns which were required to send loads of woven mantles, warriors' uniforms and shields, strings of jade beads, bundles of green feathers, lip-plugs of crystal and gold, and loads of cacao beans. The annotations are in Spanish

prisoners for sacrifice. If so, the policy turned out to be mis-guided, for the Tlaxcalans allied themselves with the Spaniards, and their support helped to bring about the destruction of Tenochtitlán.

2

The People

Physical appearance

The Aztecs were short and stocky, the men rarely more than 5 feet 6 inches tall and the women more delicately built with an average height of about 4 feet 8 inches. Skin colour varied from dark to light brown, and the typical Aztec face was broad with a prominent, and often hooked, nose (5). Eyes were black or brown almond-shaped, and frequently with epicanthic folds at the outer corners, one indication that the ancestors of the Mexicans had migrated into the New World from Asia in the long-distant past.

Hair was coarse, black, and straight. Men usually wore it cut in a fringe over the forehead and allowed it to grow to the level of the nape of the neck at the back, but the priests had their own distinctive hair style and the warriors wore pigtails and various kinds of scalp lock. The women let their hair grow long. Normally it was allowed to hang loose, but on festival days it was braided with ribbons. A more elaborate coiffure was created by binding the hair into two plaits which were wound round the head with the ends projecting like two little horns above the eyebrows (7).

Hair on the face was considered unpleasant, but nature collaborated with art by endowing the men with only meagre beards. Shaving was therefore unnecessary; facial hair was plucked out with tweeezers, and, as a further aid towards good looks, Aztec mothers applied hot cloths to the faces of their young sons in order to stifle the hair follicles and inhibit the growth of whiskers. Only old or distinguished men (who could afford to ignore fashion) wore beards, and these were at best thin and wispy.

Both men and women had great powers of endurance, and

from childhood the ordinary people had been used to hard physical work. Even the women were accustomed to walk great distances, following the menfolk and carrying a share of equipment as well as the newest baby.

People of importance prided themselves on their deportment, and tried always to move gracefully, accompanying their conversation with dignified gestures and assuming an expression appropriate to the occasion.

For a sixteenth-century Spanish description we can turn to the Anonymous Conqueror:

5 A descendant of the Aztecs. Indian woman from central Mexico

The people of this land are well made, rather tall than short. They are swarthy as leopards, of good manners and gestures, for the greater part very skilful, robust, and tireless, and at the same time the most moderate men known. They are very warlike and face death with the greatest resolution.

Personal Cleanliness

Andres de Tapia comments (with some astonishment) that Montezuma washed his body twice a day, but this love of personal cleanliness was general among the Aztecs, and everybody bathed frequently in the rivers and lakes. True soap was unknown, but among the substitutes available were the fruit of the soap-tree and the roots of certain plants which could produce a lather.

Besides these cold-water baths, a kind of sauna or steam bath was in use everywhere in the Valley of Mexico. Almost every dwelling had its bath-house, a little hemispherical building shaped rather like an igloo with a low doorway. Against it was constructed a fire-place, and the blaze warmed the adjacent wall of the bath-house until it glowed red-hot. At this stage, the bather crept into the house and threw water onto the hot wall until the interior was filled with steam. To increase the flow of perspiration and to gain full benefit from the treatment, the bather switched himself with twigs or bundles of grass. 'Soap' was used for washing, and the process might be completed with a massage, followed by a period of relaxation, lying stretched out on a mat. Both men and women used the steam baths, not only for ritual purifications and the treatment of certain diseases but as a normal part of everyday hygiene.

Cosmetics

The Aztec skin was naturally brown or bronze-coloured, but the fashionable shade for a woman's complexion was yellow. To achieve this effect the cheeks were either rubbed with a yellow earth or anointed with a cream containing *axin*, a waxy yellowish substance obtained by cooking and crushing the bodies of fat-producing insects. Travellers also used *axin* ointment as a salve to prevent the lips from cracking in frosty weather, and to protect the skin from the effect of cold.

Sahagún has left a description of the kind of make-up worn by fashion-conscious women, in particular by the courtesans who were the companions of the young warriors:

> Their faces were painted with dry, coloured powder; faces were coloured with yellow ochre, or with bitumen. Feet were anointed with an unguent of burned copal incense and dye. . . . Some cut their hair short, so that their hair reached their noses. It was cut and dyed with black mud—so did they place importance upon their heads; it was dyed with indigo, so that their hair shone. The teeth were stained with cochineal; the hands and neck were painted with designs.

Perfumes, rose water and incense were popular, and a kind of chewing gum (made of chicle mixed with *axin* and bitumen) was used to sweeten the breath. As always, the appearance and manners of the young people did not meet with the approval of the older generation, and this father's admonition to his daughter has a familiar ring: 'Never make up your face nor paint it; never put red on your mouth to look beautiful. Make-up and paint are things that light women use—shameless creatures. If you want your husband to love you, dress well, wash yourself and wash your clothes.'

30

Men painted their faces and bodies on ceremonial occasions, but it is not certain whether the Aztecs followed the example of their Otomí neighbours who covered their arms and chests with tattooed designs. Sahagún reports, however, that the fifth month of the year was the time when incisions were made on the chests of children as a mark of citizenship or tribal identification.

6 Obsidian mirror in a wooden frame. Diameter $10\frac{1}{4}$ inches

Mirrors were made from pieces of burnished iron pyrites or from obsidian, a kind of black volcanic glass which was cut and polished into discs up to a foot in diameter. These were provided with wooden frames or with loops of cord so that they could be hung on the wall (6).

Dress

The basic item of male attire, for sleep as well as for day wear, was the loincloth, a strip of fabric which went around the waist, between the legs, and was knotted so that one end hung down in front and the other behind. Its quality varied according to the wealth and status of the wearer; farmers and workmen wore simple white strips of maguey fibre cloth, while the nobility wore more elaborate versions made of cotton and embroidered with colourful patterns. Sometimes the ends were trimmed with fur, or decorated with feathers and discs of precious stone. Boys were put into loincloths at the age of four, and thereafter dressed in the same way as adults.

Poor men and manual workers wore no other garment but a loincloth. Anyone who could afford it, however, also put on a rectangular cloak which was wound round the body under the left armpit, and then knotted over the right shoulder, for buttons and pins were unknown. When a man sat down, he slipped his cloak round so that nearly all the material hung in front and covered up his body and legs(18). Rich men who owned many cloaks would advertise their wealth by wearing several at a time, one on top of the other. Ordinary men wore plain white mantles, but the courtiers and members of the upper classes dressed in cloaks woven with geometric or striped designs, dyed in bright colours, and decorated with animal and floral motifs. Montezuma's wardrobe included an orange cape with a wind-jewel design and a border of feathers, another of 'dark green, diagonally divided, in the middle of which stood an obsidian eagle', also a carmine-coloured mantle with a border of eyes, a cloak made of white duck feathers ornamented with a wolf's head pattern, a coyote fur cape with a spiral border, and a great many others, all made of luxury materials and decorated with patterns depicting shells, flowers, butterflies, and serpent or animal masks. In bad weather the Emperor wore a specially large cape to protect himself from the rain.

Priests and warriors sometimes wore a short tunic reaching to the hips or the knees, and in a bas-relief the Emperor Tizoc is shown in a symbolic battle scene wearing a thigh-length triangular apron(41). This garment may have been part of the royal war uniform, for Sahagún reports that Montezuma put on a similar apron made of quetzal feathers when he arrayed himself for battle (*see also* 39).

The principal woman's garment was a skirt which reached almost to the ankles and was held at the waist by an embroidered belt. In its everyday form the skirt was a length of plain white cloth, but for festivals and public dances the women put on their best skirts embroidered with designs of reeds, dahlias and thistles, or with patterns representing smoke, houses, animals, and fishes.

Over the skirt, women of the nobility and upper classes wore a kind of blouse made from a straight length of cloth doubled over and sewn up the sides, leaving the armholes open. The blouse fell to the hips and was usually ornamented at the neck and the lower border(7). Holiday clothes were brighter and more elaborate, made of fur or of soft cotton.

The common people went barefoot, but soldiers and richer citizens wore sandals with soles made of leather or vegetable fibre. The sandals were held in place by straps which passed

7 Inside the hut of a peasant family. The woman kneeling at the right is grinding maize while her companion on the left pats the dough into tortillas which are cooked on the pottery disc over the fire. The third woman carries a broom made from a bundle of twigs

between the big and first toes, but some kinds also had heel-guards and a complicated arrangement of straps wound round the leg in a crisscross fashion from the ankle to the knee.

The Mexicans loved display and were uninhibited in their use of jewellery and such accessories as fans, fly-whisks, and head-dresses made of green or red feathers. Beads were made of rare stones or of gold cast into the form of crabs, scorpions, birds, or sea shells, and necklaces were hung with bells which tinkled when the wearer moved. The same materials were used for pendants and chest ornaments(8), and the limbs of rich young men were adorned with leather or gold bands set with jade and turquoise mosaic. Poorer folk wore ornaments of a similar kind, but substituted shells or less expensive stones for the precious materials used by the aristocracy.

Boys had their ear-lobes perforated during childhood, and the holes were fitted with tiny plugs which were replaced by larger ones as the boy grew older. In this way the lobes were gradually stretched until the ears were capable of taking full-sized ear-spools. Each spool had a short cylindrical shaft which passed through the hole in the lobe and was attached to a flared orna-mental disc on the outside and to a holding-disc on the inside.

33

Rods of gold or precious stone were inserted through the septum of the nose, and the wings of the nostrils were pierced for the attachment of nose-studs. The lower lip was also pierced to take a labret or lip-plug (54).

The Aztecs set great store by rank and position in society. It was not enough in itself for a man to be rich or to be the holder of an important office; the fact had to be advertised publicly by means of special privileges, particularly the right to wear certain kinds of garments and insignia. Thus, turquoise was the royal colour—the equivalent of Roman purple—and only the ruler was allowed to put on a cloak of this colour or to wear a nose ornament made of turquoise. The imperial diadem was encrusted with the same material. A chief wore a leather head-band from which hung a pair of tassels, while an administrative official had a diadem made of gold and studded with jade or turquoise as his badge of rank. Anyone usurping an honour which was not his due was punished with death.

The importance of costume as an indicator of status can best be appreciated by following the career of a young warrior. As a child his scalp was shaved, but between the ages of 10 and 15 he wore a single tuft of hair at the back of the head. The young man was not allowed to remove this tuft until he had taken his first captive in battle. Then, if he had taken his prisoner single-handed, he was given the title of 'leading youth' or 'captor' and brought before the ruler to receive gifts as a sign of favour. He was allowed to dress in patterned cloaks, and to wear his hair in a new style with a single lock over the right ear. When he had taken four prisoners, he was permitted to cut his hair in the style of the seasoned warriors and was admitted to a select group with its own titles and privileges. He became one of the great captains, with the right to wear elongated labrets, leather ear-plugs, and head-bands ornamented with tassels of eagle feathers. Each further triumph brought with it new honours with their appropriate status symbols.

For the annual dance of the warriors, held in the eighth month of the year, the young men put on their finest clothes, and each wore the insignia of his rank; the captains carried standards in the form of trees, made of eagle feathers bound with ocelot fur and red cord, while the warriors who had taken captives bore on their shoulders devices in the form of birds. The leaders wore lip-plugs shaped like plants and animals, and around their necks were leather gorgets trimmed with marine shells which shone against their bronze skins. In contrast, young recruits and those who had taken no prisoners had to be content with common shells and simple disc-shaped labrets.

This emphasis on outward show made a person's achievements obvious to everybody. On the other hand, it also publicly demonstrated his shortcomings. A warrior who had taken part in three or four campaigns without capturing a prisoner was not allowed to cut off his pigtail and had to put up with the taunts of his companions who called after him, 'Big tuft of hair on the back of the head', and other hurtful remarks which made him feel ashamed. The Aztec system, which glorified success, was cruel to the failures of society.

The Aztec character

Alonso de Zorita wrote of the Mexicans: 'These people are by nature very long-suffering, and nothing will excite or anger them. They are very obedient and teachable. . . . The more noble they are, the more humility they display.' This description suggests a meek and spineless people, very different from the Aztecs of popular imagination who are forever shedding blood on either the altar or the battlefield. The contradiction, however, is more apparent than real.

On the one hand the Mexicans showed what Parry has called 'a very high degree of social docility—the willing submergence of the individual in the personality of the tribe', but against this must be set a streak of personal individualism with a tendency towards violence and extremism.

In a military state like Tenochtitlán physical bravery was taken for granted, and death in battle was something to look forward to. As a Mexican poet put it:

> There is nothing like death in war,
> nothing like the flowery death
> so precious to Him who gives life:
> far off I see it: my heart yearns for it!

Success in war had given the Aztecs more than a fair share of national pride, and the arrogance of Mexican officials and tax-gatherers was notorious. The structure and values of society were designed to foster competition and pride in achievement, and the Aztecs were clearly not lacking in ambition and self-esteem, nor apparently in passion, for the severe penalties for adultery and drunkenness—both of which are crimes of excess—suggest that these were two evils which could only be kept down by repression.

A well-bred Aztec was, however, expected to exercise self-control and to behave with dignity. Sahagún has left a word-portrait of the perfect nobleman, a person who is serious and modest, who 'wishes no praise', who is 'solicitous of others', chaste and devout, eloquent but discreet in his conversation, diligent, wise, polite, 'a follower in the ways of his parents', and an example to other people. This, of course, is an idealized picture, and the high standard of behaviour may have been more often sought after than achieved.

The same emphasis on moderation, responsibility, and self-restraint is found in the *Precepts of the Elders*, a class of literature written in a high-flown and wordy style to instruct young people in behaviour and manners. Here is one Aztec father talking to his son:

> Revere and greet your elders; console the poor and the afflicted with good works and words. . . . Follow not the madmen who honour neither father nor mother; for they are like animals, for they neither take nor hear advice. . . . Do not mock the old, the sick, the maimed, or one who has sinned. Do not insult or abhor them, but abase yourself before God and fear lest the same befall you. . . . Do not set a bad example, or speak indiscreetly, or interrupt the speech of another. If someone does not speak well or coherently, see that you do not the same; if it is not your business to speak, be silent. If you are asked something, reply soberly and without affectation or flattery or prejudice to others, and your speech will be well regarded. . . . Wherever you go, walk with a peaceful air, and do not make wry faces or improper gestures.
>
> (Zorita)

There is much more in the same vein, and near the end—inevitably—comes the sentence which every young man has heard at some time or other: 'Son, if you do not heed your father's advice, you will come to a bad end, and the fault will be yours.'

The Mexicans were addicted to making speeches and giving advice, often at great length, and many of their songs and poems have a philosophical theme which gives further insight into the

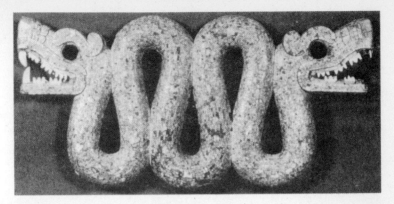

8 Pectoral ornament in the shape of a double-headed serpent.
Turquoise mosaic on a wooden base

Aztec temperament. One obsession is with the transitory nature
of life and the difficulty of finding anything permanent on
earth:

> It is not true, it is not true
> that we come on this earth to live.
> We come only to sleep, only to dream.
> Our body is a flower.
> As grass becomes green in the springtime,
> So our hearts will open and give forth buds
> and then they wither.

Even the search for philosophical truth ends only in failure
and doubt.

> How many can truthfully say
> that truth is or is not there?

Some people found a solution in epicureanism, the enjoyment of life while it lasts, but even their pleasure was tinged
with melancholy:

> Only in passing are we here on earth.
> In peace and pleasure let us spend our lives;
> come let us enjoy ourselves.
> . . . Would that one lived forever;
> Would that one were not to die!

The same fatalistic acceptance can be seen in man's relationship with the gods, when the love of pageantry and ceremony

which affected every part of Aztec life reached its climax in the ritual of worship.

Generalizations about national character are always dangerous and likely to be misleading, but the typical Aztec (who must have been as rare as the typical Englishman) seems to have been a good citizen, rather conservative and tied to tradition, with his competitive and aggressive instincts held in check by good manners and self-control, ceremonious in his dealings with other people, sensitive to beauty and to the symbolism which underlies philosophy and religion, inclined to be pompous and perhaps a bit humourless, honest and hard-working, proud of his position in society, superstitious and fatalistic in his attitude towards life.

Food and drink

Cattle and other large meat-producing animals were introduced to the Americas by the European conquerors, and meat was therefore a luxury for the ordinary family in Aztec times. Fortunately Mexico is a land rich in vegetable foods and these formed the main items on the everyday menu.

The preparation of maize was a daily task for the housewife, and even now in country parts of Mexico it still occupies up to six hours of a woman's day. The kernels were steeped in lime overnight to loosen the hull, then boiled and skinned, and finally ground to flour by crushing between a grooved stone roller and a *metate* (a stone slab standing on three little legs)(7). The maize was usually made into tortillas, thin round cakes of unleavened meal baked on flat clay griddles about a foot in diameter. Tortillas become dry and inedible after a few hours and were accordingly made fresh for each meal. The daily ration for a three-year-old child was half a tortilla, and the amount was gradually increased until a five-year-old had a whole tortilla to himself and by the age of 13 was eating two per day.

Maize was also made into a sort of porridge called *atole* which was seasoned with pimento or sweetened with either honey or a syrup made from the sap of the maguey plant. Another favourite dish was *tamales*, envelopes of steamed maize stuffed with savoury vegetables or meat. Sahagún lists more than 40 different shapes and fillings, and some of the recipes are unexpected, to say the least. The tamales filled with mush-rooms, fruit, fish, rabbit, beans, turkey eggs, or green and red peppers are appetizing enough, but the European stomach quails at the thought of some of the others—the frog tamales, for example, or those containing snails, beeswax, tadpoles, or axolotls (an immature form of salamander which looks rather like a newt).

Tenochtitlán was a lakeside city, and from the time of their arrival in the swamps, when poverty compelled them to eat anything they could get, the Mexicans had consumed all kinds of water creatures. Fish were an important source of protein, but shrimps and the larvae of water flies were also collected, and insect eggs were skimmed from the surface and eaten like caviar. Things of this sort were the food of the poor and a standby in times of shortage, but some of the items were also regarded as delicacies. Axolotls with yellow peppers were a dish fit for the ruler's table.

Grubs were extracted from the fleshy leaves of the maguey cactus, and at certain times of the year the Mexicans collected a species of ant which becomes swollen with honey. The farmers grew every sort of fruit, as well as tomatoes, amaranth, sage, avocados, and several varieties of beans. The Mexicans also gathered mushrooms, wild fruits, and all kinds of green-stuff.

The lake abounded in waterfowl, and if a hunter were lucky he might bring home a deer or a peccary, though his bag was more likely to be a rabbit, a hare, a gopher, or a pigeon. The Aztecs despised the Otomí of the hill country who ate 'unclean' creatures like lizards, rats, and snakes.

The only domestic sources of meat were turkeys and the edible dogs which were specially fattened for the table by forced feeding, and were of a hairless breed which is now almost extinct. They were unable to bark, and the Spanish chronicler, Father Clavigero, describes them as 'sad-faced and uncom-plaining, even when beaten'. For the farmer and the city workman poultry or dog flesh was a luxury to be eaten only on special occasions.

The family generally rose at dawn and worked without eating until about ten o'clock when it was time for the first meal, which for the common man was usually no more than a dish of maize porridge. A man working a long way from home made do with a cold meal prepared by his wife, but for those in the house the main meal came during the hottest part of the day and, at least among the leisured classes, was often followed by a siesta. Food was usually roasted, grilled, or boiled. For the ordinary people even the main meal of the day was a simple affair of tortillas or maize cakes with beans and perhaps a spicy sauce of tomatoes or chilli peppers, for the Aztecs, like their present-day descendants, enjoyed highly seasoned food. The midday meal was also the last, except for a bowl of gruel made from amaranth, sage, or maize, which was taken just before going to bed.

In the house of a peasant or workman mealtime was just a brief interlude in the day's routine. The members of the family squatted round the fire (for there was no table) and ate quickly, using rolled tortillas as spoons. If guests were present, the womenfolk served all the men first and had their own meal only after the men had finished.

The Anonymous Conqueror noted that 'these people live with very little food, as little perhaps as any people in the world', but the nobles, rich merchants, and the better-off craftsmen fared very differently. Their meals were more elaborate, and for them the night was a time for feasting and party-giving. It was people like these who could afford the pineapples and chocolate which were traded from the hot lands of Vera Cruz and who bought the oysters and crabs, the turtles and sea fish which were imported from the coast.

Bernal Díaz has left a first-hand description of the mealtime of Montezuma. The ruler sat behind a screen at a table covered with fine white cloths. Before the food was served, four clean and beautiful girls brought water for his hands while others brought maize cakes.

> For each meal his cooks made him more than 30 different dishes prepared according to their style and custom, and underneath them they put small earthenware braziers to prevent the food from getting cold. They cooked more than 300 plates of the food the great Montezuma was going to eat, and over 1,000 more for the guard.

In spite of this vast menu, Montezuma himself seems to have been an abstemious man, for the author records that he ate only a little of the fruit which was offered to him for dessert and was equally sparing with the chocolate which followed the main courses.

We can get some idea of what went into the Emperor's 30 dishes from the writings of Sahagún. Among the Mexican delicacies he describes are locusts with sage, fish with chilli peppers and tomatoes, prickly pears with fish eggs, frogs with green chillis, venison with red chilli, tomatoes and ground squash seeds, and duck stewed in a pot. Gourd seeds, roasted and salted like peanuts at the present day, were nibbled as a snack.

Water was the normal drink of the poor, but the rich could afford to buy chocolate which was very highly esteemed (the name itself is an Anglicized version of the Mexican word *chocolatl*). The cacao nuts were pounded, and then boiled in water with a little maize flour. The oil was skimmed off, the mixture strained into a vessel, and whipped up into a stiff froth which gradually dissolved in the mouth. It was generally consumed cold, often flavoured with honey, vanilla, or various spices.

An alcoholic drink called *octli* was made from the fermented sap of the maguey plant. Aztec law was particularly severe towards drunkards, but some indulgence was shown towards old men and women on the grounds that 'their blood was turning cold', and they were allowed to drink *octli*, and even to get a little drunk, on certain holidays. At weddings and festivals there was a general dispensation and all persons over 30 years old were permitted to drink. In theory the ration was two goblets per person, but no doubt this rule was broken more often than it was observed. Porters and men engaged in heavy work were allowed to refresh themselves occasionally, and women were given *octli* as a tonic in the days immediately after childbirth.

A more dangerous kind of intoxication was produced by drugs like *peyotl* (from the buds of a cactus which grows in the deserts of northern Mexico) and a bitter black mushroom called *teonanacatl*, 'sacred fungus' or 'flesh of the gods', which was sometimes served with honey at feasts and banquets. Both these drugs produce hallucinations. Peyotl, the source of the drug mescalin, intensifies visual impressions and causes coloured hallucinations, while *teonanacatl* may produce, in a mild form, the symptoms of madness with all kinds of visions and illusions. People who ate the mushroom had comic visions or saw terrifying things like snakes. Some thought their bodies were full of worms which ate them alive. Others laughed hysterically or hid themselves away, and a few even hanged themselves or threw themselves over cliffs. The seeds of climbing convolvulus (known in England as Morning Glory, but called by the Mexicans *ololiuhqui* or 'holy plant') were taken for their hallucinatory effects and were used in medical diagnosis.

A less violent satisfaction came from tobacco which is native to the New World and was smoked by the richer Mexicans at the end of the meal. The tobacco was mixed with pulverized charcoal, to which were added flowers, powdered bitumen, and other aromatic substances, and was smoked in tube-shaped pipes made out of hollow reeds or from more expensive materials like tortoiseshell, silver, or painted and gilded wood. The Aztecs compressed the nostrils with the fingers while inhaling the smoke, and Díaz describes how Montezuma, having finished his evening meal, would take his chocolate as he watched his dwarfs and dancers perform (16), and would then smoke for a little while before going to sleep.

Games and pastimes

The most important sport in Mexico was the ball game which the Aztecs, who saw the will of the gods in almost everything, invested with a religious significance. It was played in a court laid out in the form of a capital 'I' with exaggerated cross-pieces. The central section measured 200 feet or more in length by about 30 in width, and was enclosed by walls some 15 feet high and made of masonry faced with stucco (9). From the mid-point of each side-wall a stone ring (with a hole just big enough to allow the six-inch rubber ball to pass through) projected at right angles over the body of the court at a height of about 10 feet above the ground. The floor was of smooth plaster, and in the Codex Mendoza is shown divided into four quarters each of a different colour.

The more usual arrangement was a division into two fields by means of a line drawn across the floor of the court from ring to ring. The aim of the players was to propel the ball backwards and forwards across this line, and a point was scored if one team managed to drive the ball into the cross-piece of the opponents' court. The players were allowed to use only their hips, knees, and elbows, and since the ball was made of solid rubber they protected themselves against its impact by wearing

9 Ball game. The rings, here shown outside the court, in fact projected inwards at right angles to the side-walls (Codex Magliabecchiano)

belts of leather stuffed with cotton. Pads were also worn on the hands and knees because a player often had to fling himself on the ground in the attempt to take an awkward return. In spite of these precautions, players sometimes died of exhaustion or were so badly bruised about the hips that they had to be bled by the doctors.

If any player managed to drive the ball through one of the rings his team won outright, and as a reward the man was allowed to confiscate the clothes and possessions of all the spectators. This was not an easy custom to enforce, and everybody scrambled for the exit while the player and his friends tried to grab as many people as they could.

Although the ball game was played only by noblemen and by professionals in the employ of the ruler and his courtiers, it had the spectator appeal of a football match or a race meeting today. People came to watch, to bet, and to forget about more serious matters; and a shrewd ruler 'when he beheld and knew that the common folk and vassals were very fretful, then commanded that the ball game should be played in order to animate the people and divert them' (Sahagún).

On a symbolic level, the court represented the universe and the ball stood for the sun, moon, or one of the planets. The game itself was sacred to the gods and formed part of a number of religious ceremonies. The courts were usually close to the most important temples, and in Tenochtitlán two ball courts dedicated to the sun and moon were among the buildings in the Temple Precinct.

The game was also used in divination, as a sort of trial by contest. Nezahualhilli of Texcoco once staked his kingdom against three turkeycocks in a match with Montezuma to determine whether Texcocan astrologers had spoken the truth when they prophesied that strangers would soon rule over Mexico. The first two games went to Montezuma, but Nezahualpilli won the next three to take the set. The Aztec ruler, we may imagine, left the court a very worried man—and it was not long before the prediction was proved true.

Another favourite pastime was *patolli*, a game like backgammon, played on a mat painted with a design resembling a St Andrew's cross divided up into sections or 'houses', some of which bore special markings to indicate either safe ground or areas which incurred a penalty. Instead of dice the Aztecs threw four or five black beans with the numbers indicated by holes in the faces. Twelve counters (six red and six blue) were divided among the players who moved them round the course according to the number which came up. Throws of 5 and 10 counted double, and there seems to have been some provision for capturing an opponent's man. According to Clavigero, the

10 Gamblers playing *patolli*. The players offer prayers to the god Five Flower who is shown watching over the game
(Codex Magliabecchiano)

game was won by the player who first got three counters in a row, and Sahagún records that if any of the beans stood up on its end the player who threw it won outright, whatever the score at the time.

Patolli, like the ball game, had a religious significance and was symbolic of the 52-year cycle, but its greatest attraction was for gamblers who wagered jewels, clothes, slaves, and houses on the result. The players spoke to the beans, rubbing them between their hands for luck, and burned incense to Macuilxochitl (Five Flower), the god of gambling (10). Some men became so addicted to the game that they carried *patolli* sets with them everywhere, and many people were ruined by their passion for it.

Another entertainment charged with religious symbolism was the *volador*. A tall pole was set up with a movable

11 Volador ceremony, from a manuscript of the early Spanish period

platform at the top, and four men dressed as birds attached themselves by long ropes to the corners of the frame. At a signal they all leaped off, and as the rope unwound the platform rotated and caused the four 'birds' to fly round and round the pole (11). The lengths of the ropes were adjusted so that each player made 13 circuits before reaching the ground, giving a total of 52 revolutions which symbolized the years of the Calendar Round (pp. 168–170).

Music and dancing

The Aztec orchestra included only a few instruments capable of sustaining a melody, but had a strong and varied percussion section. Music therefore tended to be rhythmic rather than tuneful, with a great reliance on drums and rattles.

The base part was taken by the *huehuetl*, a vertical drum made from a hollowed log 2–4 feet high and about 12–18 inches in diameter. The bottom of the drum was cut away in a step pattern to form three flange-shaped legs, and the top was covered with hide or snakeskin. The sides of the finest drums were carved with scenes in low relief (12). These vertical drums could be tuned, and the tone was raised by warming the instrument close to a brazier. They were normally beaten with the hands, and Díaz observed that the temple drums made a 'sad sound' which could be heard six miles away. Smaller versions of the *huehuetl* were hung round the neck or held under the arm for dancing.

A lighter note was produced by the *teponaztli*, a wooden gong which was carefully constructed in the form of a horizontal cylinder with two longitudinal tongues cut in the top (13). The ends of the cylinder were left solid, but the base was open and was occasionally attached to a soundboard. Gongs of this kind were struck with drum-sticks tipped with rubber, and were carefully carved so that each tongue gave out a different note. The *teponaztli* was a high-toned tenor instrument, useful both in the orchestra and for providing a rhythm accompaniment to songs and poems. The musician either placed the gong on a waist-high stand or sat down with the instrument resting in front of him on a twist of cloth or rope to raise it clear of the ground. Aztec gongs were often made in the shape of animals or human beings, while those from the Mixtec lands were more frequently carved with

12 Wooden upright drum carved in relief, from Toluca

46

13 Two-tone wooden gong

mythological or religious scenes very similar in style to those of the manuscript books.

A different kind of drum was made from a tortoise or turtle shell. Rattles were of clay or of wood carved into various complicated shapes (17), and the percussion section also included dried gourds containing seeds or pebbles which made a swishing noise when shaken. The largest instrument of the rattle family consisted of a staff hung with bells and wooden discs which clashed together when the butt of the pole was banged on the ground. Another rhythm instrument was the rasp made of a notched bone which was scraped with a stick or the edge of a shell. To add to the effect, dancers attached copper bells to their clothing (55) and wore strings of jangling objects such as shells, little bones, or dried nuts.

Stringed instruments were unknown, and the melodic line was taken by the flutes. These were usually made of clay (more rarely of bamboo or bone), were about 6–8 inches long and could play only a limited number of notes (14). The most common number is five, which suggests that Aztec musicians employed a five-note scale, but they also used double and triple flutes which had as many as 16 stops altogether. Pan pipes were known, and some of them could play chords, but Aztec melodies must have been of a fairly simple kind.

Conch-shell trumpets, whose mournful note could be varied by altering the strength of the blast, were used to signal the start of festivals, to clear the way for processions (27), and to rouse the city in the early mornings. Clay whistles shaped like animals and human beings may have been children's toys, but

47

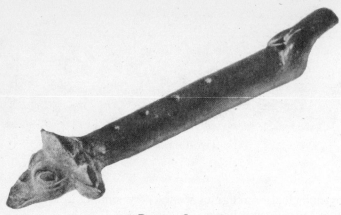

14 Pottery flute

similar instruments (often with several stops) were used in battle to give signals and to confuse the enemy.

One of the most important instruments is, of course, the human voice. In ancient Mexico, singing, instrumental music and dancing were so intimately linked that it is impossible to discuss one without reference to the others. Orchestral 'performances' in which the musicians played to a non-participating audience were rare, and, as we have seen, the Aztec orchestra was by its composition ill suited for such a task (15). The strong rhythm section, however, was ideal for beating time for dancers and for supporting choruses or individual singers, and all these musical activities played a vital part in Mexican life.

Singing, dancing, and theatrical performances were among the favourite Aztec amusements, and troupes of professionals were attached to all the richest households. Visitors were entertained with music, dancing, mimes, poetry-recitals, and plays in which the actors put on special costumes to declaim their parts. The different tribes or regions of the Empire all had their own songs and styles of singing, and when a piece from another province was performed the musicians dressed in the appropriate costumes and copied the mannerisms of the people they were mimicking. Interspersed with the serious items were comic turns performed by clowns, dwarfs, hunchbacks, jugglers, stilt-dancers, and acrobats who danced with other men balanced on their shoulders (16).

48

15 Aztec orches-
tra, with upright
drum, two-tone
wooden gong, and
several rattles
(Codex
Florentino)

Musical standards in Montezuma's palace must have been high, for Sahagún's description of a royal feast concludes with these words:

> And if the singers did something amiss—perchance a *teponaztli* was out of tune, or a ground drum; or he who intoned the song spoiled it; or the leader marred the dance—then the ruler commanded that they place in jail whoever had done the wrong; they imprisoned him, and he died.

Music played an integral part in the education of a nobleman or priest. It is clear that individuals sang and played for their own private enjoyment, but Aztec music was above all social and communal, with the mass participation of singers and dancers. The great popular festivals served a useful purpose in allowing the people to work off tensions and surplus energy through dances and chanting, but they had a second, and more serious, function. The dancing and the singing gave pleasure, but at the same time they brought man and the gods closer together. There is no contradiction in this, for our own Christmas festivities and Mardi Gras carnivals show the same blend of sacred purpose and physical enjoyment. The carols and the oratorios are the modern counterpart of the chants sung at the Aztec religious festivals, and the analogy helps to explain why music and the correct observance of traditional rites were of such importance in Mexican life.

As the Spanish friar, Motolinía, put it:

> In these religious festivals and their dances, they not only called on
> and honoured and praised their gods with songs, but also with the
> heart and with movements of the body. In order to do so properly,
> they had and used many patterns, not only in the movements of
> the head, of the arms and of the feet, but with all their body.

In the eleventh month, the people assembled in the square at
sunset for the 'handwaving' dance in which four rows of
performers circled round in silence without any musical
accompaniment. There was also a 'serpent' dance in which the
warriors and young women joined hands, and another dance
in which the noblemen of Tenochtitlán and Tlatelolco faced
each other in two rows. Many of the religious dances would be
better described as dance-dramas in which priests or god-
impersonators took the solo parts and the congregation played
the part of both chorus and corps de ballet.

Besides the religious dances there were also secular dances in
which as many as 4,000 people took part. Durán describes a
provocative and indecent dance which he compares to a
saraband, and there were others in which the performers
clasped each other round the waist or neck. In yet another of
these secular dances the participants linked arms and formed
up into two long lines, each of which was led by an experienced
dancer who decided on the steps which the others had to copy.
Sometimes he imitated the mannerisms of foreigners, women, or
drunks, and he introduced many changes of tempo to keep the
dancers alert. This dance was accompanied by singing, with the
two leaders chanting the verses and everybody joining in the
choruses.

Music was not written down, and not a single Aztec tune has
been preserved. In Tenochtitlán were special academies where
boys and girls were taught by trained instructors how to sing,
dance, and play musical instruments, but there was no clear
distinction between the musical and the literary arts. Aztec
poetry was meant to be sung or declaimed against a musical
background rather than to be recited, and above the text of
certain poems is a notation giving the rhythm of the *teponaztli*
which was to accompany the verses. Even the words for 'poem'
and 'song' have the same linguistic root.

From a study of the words of the songs it is evident how much the music and dancing reflected Aztec religious beliefs and national aspirations. For this reason the Spaniards did their best to discourage the native musical tradition, and as late as 1555 (31 years after the Conquest) it was still found necessary to issue the following ordinance:

> The Indians shall not sing the said chants of their rites or ancient histories, without first having the said chants examined by the Clergy, or by people that understand the language very well. The ministers of the Gospel shall see that there is nothing profane in such chants.

16 The amusements of the nobility; a performance by musicians, a juggler, hunchbacks, and a dwarf (Codex Florentino)

Language and oral literature

The Nahuatl language is pleasant to listen to, easy to pronounce, and equipped with a rich vocabulary. It shares with such languages as Greek and German the habit of building up long, compound words by a process which M. León-Portilla has described as *linguistic engineering*—a kind of language structure which makes it easy to create abstract terms in which philosophical or poetic ideas can be expressed.

The spoken language is therefore a tool of great flexibility, but unfortunately the Aztec system of writing was inadequate for the task of transcribing any sort of complex or abstract theme. As Antonio de Herrera, chronicler to King Philip II, perceptively remarked:

> . . . because their characters were not sufficient, like our own writing, they could not set things down exactly, only the substance of their ideas; but they learned in chorus many speeches, orations and songs. They took great care to see that the youths learned them by memory, and for this they had schools in which the old taught them to the group. By this means the texts were preserved in their entirety.

17 Carved wooden terrapin 3¼ inches long. It once formed the head of a staff or rattle

Learning by heart was therefore an important part of a child's education, especially for a child in the *telpochcalli* school where reading and writing were not taught.

It was in any case quite impracticable to use hieroglyphs for writing down poetry with its subtleties of thought and language. In the absence of such books it was therefore the oral rather than the written tradition which kept Nahuatl literature alive by passing down the most famous songs and speeches from one generation to the next. As Nezahualcoyotl expressed it in one of his verses,

> My flowers shall not cease to live;
> my songs shall never end:
> I, the singer, intone them;
> they become scattered, they are spread about.

The poem must have been composed before the king's death in 1472, but it was still being sung in the sixteenth century when the Spaniards introduced the alphabet and made it possible to write down Nahuatl texts for the first time.

About 2,000 different works have been preserved in this way. They include hymns, verse epics, lyrical poems praising the beauty of flowers or lamenting the transience of human life, dramatic poetry and fragments of theatrical works, songs about Aztec legends and history, and items dealing with philosophical themes, news events (such as plagues, comets, or hunting incidents), and comic or indecent subjects. The main categories of prose work were the historical annals and the so-called *Precepts of the Elders* whose dreary pages were filled with speeches of advice to young people.

As we have seen, poetry was meant to be sung or declaimed. The manner of performance has left its mark on the structure of the verse, and Mexican poetry shares the characteristics common to oral literature all over the world. Such well-tried devices as repetition, parallelism, and the use of refrains are found wherever the oral tradition predominates over the written one (in the psalms, for instance, but also in operatic arias, folk songs, political speeches, and nursery rhymes) and they have the dual function of making the verses easier to remember and at the same time slowing down the narrative so that the audience has plenty of time to grasp the sense of it.

Nahuatl poetry did not rhyme. It gained its effect from the rhythm and balance of accented and unaccented syllables, combined with skilful use of the caesura and natural pauses. Assonance and alliteration were also popular, and the language was high-flown and poetical, full of obscure metaphors, parallelisms, and esoteric allusions. This is especially true of the hymns, which must have been incomprehensible to all but the priests and the learned. Some of these verses are no more than magical formulae, repeated over and over again with minor variations, as in this song, addressed to the maize goddess:

> O seven ears, arise, awake. Our mother, thou leavest us now;
> thou goest to thy home in Tlalocan.
> Arise, awake. Our mother, thou leavest us now;
> thou goest to thy home in Tlalocan.

> (Sahagún)

All Nahuatl poetry, religious or secular, is full of imagery. In this war poem, the battlefield is described as a place

> where the burning, divine liquor is poured out,
> where the divine eagles are blackened with smoke,
> where the tigers roar,
> where gems and rich jewels are scattered,
> where precious feathers wave like spume,
> there, where the warriors tear each other
> and noble princes are smashed to pieces.

By this accumulation of imagery the poet has captured the glitter and confusion of a Mexican battle, secure in the knowledge that his audience would recognize the allusions to the Eagle and Jaguar knights, and to the blood (the 'divine liquor') with which the gods were fed.

Another favourite procedure, used in prose as well as poetry, was to place two words or phrases next to each other in such a way as to suggest an idea which was never directly expressed.

These phrases were always used metaphorically, and, if taken literally, their meaning is distorted or lost completely:

'in the bag and in the box' = a secret
'in the clouds, in the mist' = mysteriously
'jade and fine plumes' = beauty
'stumbling-place and crossroads' = moral danger

The phrase 'flower and song' stood for poetry itself and is a recurrent metaphor in Mexican verse, as in this elegy which praises a Tenochca poet:

An emerald fell to the ground,
a flower was born; your song!
Whenever you intone your songs here in Mexico
the sun shines eternally.

Aztec speeches make dull reading today. The *Precepts of the Elders* are wordy and rhetorical, full of circumlocutions and repetitions, and heavy with the imagery and ornate phrases which were the mark of fine language. All literature, however, is the product of its time, and the simplicity and economy so admired today are in part a reflection of the speed and bustle of modern life. Aztec literature was composed for a more leisurely era, one where there was more time to sit and listen, more respect for tradition and old age, more formality in the conduct of everyday life. Our grandfathers, brought up on lengthy sermons and three-decker novels, would perhaps have felt more in sympathy with it.

After the turgid speeches it is refreshing to pick up one of the Mexican histories. The transcribed texts contain material drawn from pictographic codices, together with speeches or poetic interludes which could only have come from the oral tradition. Some of the annals, like the extract quoted below from a manuscript of 1576, are really commentaries such as an interpreter would make on a hieroglyphic codex. All the information is of the factual kind which could be expressed in pictures:

Year 10 Flint   Chimalpopoca died. The Tepanecs did away with him.
13 House: In this year the sun was eaten up (i.e. there was an eclipse): all the stars appeared. It was then that Axayácatl died.
11 Rabbit: In this year there were hailstorms. All the fish died in the water.

3

Family Life

At the age of about 20 a young man was considered ready to take on the responsibilities of adult life, which meant in effect that he should get married, for without a wife to prepare his food and to do the domestic chores he could not set up his own household. Unmarried men and women were not regarded as adult members of the community, but once a couple were married and established they became full citizens, listed on the register of householders kept by the *calpulli* scribes, and with the right to farm a plot of land from the clan holding.

The special skills of both partners were necessary for the smooth working of a marriage. The man was house-builder and farmer or craftsman; the woman prepared meals, cared for the children, wove cloth and made garments, tended the kitchen garden, and looked after the family's livestock. In the eyes of society a marriage without children was incomplete. Barrenness was therefore a social as well as a personal tragedy, and many childless marriages ended in divorce. The aims of the ordinary Mexican, man or woman, were those of people everywhere: a respected position in the community, a happy family life, and a marriage blessed with children.

Birth

The birth of a child was a cause for celebration, and its delivery was entrusted to an aged midwife who was experienced in both the medical and ritual aspects of childbirth. Every important occasion in Aztèc life was accompanied by speeches. Even the newborn child could not escape them, and while the midwife cut the umbilical cord she explained to the infant what its duties would be in life; if a boy, he would grow up to be a

55

warrior whose mission was to feed the Sun with the blood of enemies, while a girl would spend her days in household chores, helping the family and rarely going out. After submitting the baby to these speeches, the midwife gave it a cold bath, and put the swaddled infant into a cradle (7).

Meanwhile all the relatives were informed of the birth, and they assembled at the house to congratulate the mother and to look at the child. As soon as they entered the door the visitors took ashes and rubbed them on their knees and joints as a charm to prevent lameness and rheumatism in the baby. Presents were handed out and, inevitably, there were more speeches. The period of visiting lasted four days. During this time, the family carefully looked after the fire to make sure that it never went out. Nobody was allowed to remove a piece of burning wood from the house, 'lest this action take renown from the child who had been born' (Sahagún).

Sometime during the four days of celebration, the father called in an astrologer to read the child's horoscope and determine a propitious day for the naming ceremony. The Aztecs believed that the day-sign under which a child was born would influence him throughout his life. A boy born on the day 2 Rabbit would turn out to be a drunkard who would bring ruin upon himself and his family. The sign 9 Deer would make a person evil-tempered, foul-mouthed, and lazy, while a boy born under 1 Ocelot would end his days as a slave or as a captive sacrificed on the altar. Other days were considered fortunate: 10 Eagle gave strength and courage, 11 Vulture a long and happy life; 7 Flower was a good day for craftsmen; 5 Monkey gave a child the gift of entertaining and amusing others, while the infant born under the sign 4 Dog would prosper without apparent effort. Still other days could be either fortunate or unlucky. To the child born on the day 3 Water, wealth would come easily—and go just as easily: 'like water it would pass away'.

It must have been obvious that these prophecies were not always fulfilled and that the day-sign could not have been the only factor causing good or bad fortune. A person had some control over his fate. A favourable birth sign could be made ineffective by evil conduct later in life, but a person who obeyed the rules could expect a successful future. Similarly a bad sign could be redeemed by good conduct and religious observance, but, even so, a man born under an evil sign would always carry round with him a predisposition for ill luck.

The duty of the astrologer was to choose the most favourable day for the child's naming ceremony. If possible this took place four days after birth, but infants born on unlucky days were not named until fortunate ones occurred, even if this meant postponing the ceremony.

The midwife also took charge of the naming ritual. The baby was carried out into the courtyard of the house to be bathed in an earthenware tub placed on a layer of rushes. Water was sprinkled on the child's mouth, chest, and head, while the appropriate incantations were made. Then the midwife washed the baby all over and recited the prayer to keep away evil. In addition, a boy was presented to the Sun, with a prayer that he might acquit himself well as a warrior.

A male child had the symbols of his father's profession carried out to him, a miniature shield and arrows to show that he would be a warrior, and craftsman's tools if he was to enter his father's trade. His umbilical cord and his miniature weapons were entrusted to a warrior for burial far away on a battlefield. To a girl baby the midwife showed a miniature spindle, a work-basket, and a broom to symbolize her household tasks, and the infant's umbilical cord was buried in the home to show that she would not be free to wander like her brother.

The name was now announced, and the news was spread by little boys who ran through the streets shouting out the details at the tops of their voices.

Each child had a calendrical name taken from the date of his birth and also a personal name which belonged to him alone. The most famous ruler of Texcoco, for example, was usually called Nezahualcoyotl (which may be translated as Hungry Coyote), but he occasionally appears in the texts under his calendar name of Ce Mazatl, 1 Deer. Animals figure prominently in Mexican names, and the chronicles are filled with the deeds of such personages as Angry Turkey, Bee in the Reeds, Speaking Eagle, or Fire Coyote. Other men took their names from articles of clothing (Tiger Lip Plug), or from their personal qualities, like He Who laughs at Women, or the unfortunately named Moquihuix (Drunkard). Some names, such as Black Hill, have a topographical origin. Girls were given more feminine names like Jade Doll, or Precious Broken Plume of the

Quetzal Bird, which in its Nahuatl form (Tziquetzalpoztectzin) is almost as long a mouthful as in English, and flower names were especially popular—for example, Azcalxochitzin (Ant Flower), Miahuaxiuitl (Turquoise Maize-Flower) or Quiauh-xochitl (Rain Flower). All these personal names, like those of towns and cities, can be written in the form of pictograms (30).

After the naming ceremony came a banquet for all the friends and relatives of the family. Guests were garlanded with flowers and given scented tobacco to smoke while the womenfolk prepared the meal. Here was another opportunity for displays of rhetoric. All through the speeches, even on such a happy occasion, ran a note of melancholy, an emphasis on the transience of human life and on the suffering to be endured. The midwife took up the theme as soon as the infant was born—'we cannot tell if you will live long among us . . . we cannot tell what kind of fate will be yours'—and the old people continued in the same vein throughout the banquet:

> O my beloved grandson . . . thou shalt behold, come to know, and feel pain, affliction and suffering. This earth is a place of torment and affliction . . . a place of much toil and affliction. Perhaps it shall be our blessing and reward that for a little time thou shalt be lent to us. (Sahagún)

After the main courses chocolate was served, and as it grew dusk the old folk put this aside in favour of goblets of intoxicating *octli*. By late evening they were all thoroughly drunk, singing, making witty remarks, and indulging in fits of maudlin weeping, so that from outside it 'sounded as if dogs were barking'.

After 20 days, when the excitement connected with the naming had died down, the parents took the child to the temple where, with offerings of food and clothes, they presented him before the priests.

Childhood and education

At first the child was given no jobs to do but was taught by 'quiet words'. Then, at the age of four, practical instruction began and children were allowed to do simple jobs under the watchful eye of their elders. Boys were sent to fetch water, while mothers taught their daughters the names and uses of all the things in the work basket. Little by little the children were given more responsible tasks, the girls helping their mothers around the house and the boys following their fathers to work or to the market.

The education of a girl was really a training for marriage. Between the ages of five and seven she was shown how to handle a spindle and make thread, then in the early teens came instruction in cookery, and at the age of 14 she learned to weave on a loom. With marriage only two years away, a girl was by this time a young adult, trained to run a house and able to supplement the family income by weaving cloth for sale. The education of boys was equally practical. A five-year-old tottered along behind his father carrying a few sticks or a tiny bundle, and then as the years passed he learned how to catch fish, cut rushes, and handle a canoe on the lake (18).

At the same time, parents taught their children good be-haviour and made them suffer lectures on the virtues of hard work, truthfulness, respect for the aged, the necessity for self-control, obedience to authority and to the will of the gods. Lazy or defiant children were punished. Boys were beaten, pricked with maguey spines, then tied hand and foot and laid naked on the wet ground for a whole day, or else were held over a fire of chilli peppers and made to inhale the bitter smoke. Girls too were pricked or held over the fire, but they were also made to do extra housework, being forced to rise before dawn and to spend the whole day cleaning the home and sweeping the street outside (18).

The children of the nobility were most strictly brought up because in adult life they were expected to set an example to others. Boys were soon turned over to the *calmecac* school (*see* p. 64), but some girls did not leave home until the day of their wedding. The upbringing of a ruler's daughter was particularly severe, and the following account (condensed from Zorita) suggests that life in the palace was often cold and formal:

When she reached the age of four, they impressed on her the need for being very discreet in speech and conduct, in appearance and bearing. . . . A ruler's daughter went about in the company of many elderly women, and she walked so modestly that she never raised her eyes from the ground . . . she never spoke in the temple, save to say the prayers she had been taught; she must not speak while eating, but must keep absolute silence. The rule that a man, even a brother, must not speak to an unmarried woman was observed as strictly as if it were law. . . . The maidens could not go out to the gardens without guards. If they took a single step out of the door they were harshly punished, especially if they had reached the age of 10 or 12. Maidens who raised their eyes from the ground or looked behind them were also punished cruelly; the same was done to girls who were careless or lazy. They were taught how to speak to the ruler's wives and to other persons, and were punished if they showed negligence in this. They were constantly admonished to heed the good counsel they received.

When they reached the age of five, their nurses began teaching them to embroider, sew and weave, and never permitted them to be idle. A maiden (even a child) who stopped work without permission was punished.

Repression, punishment, and constant hard work are the themes which recur throughout this and similar accounts. Royal parents seem to have been distant figures who remained aloof from their children. At certain fixed hours the little girls were allowed to play in the presence of their mothers, but even then there were guards and nursemaids in the room and it was not an occasion of real family intimacy. An interview with their father was an even more cheerless experience:

When a ruler wished to see his daughters, they came as if in procession, a matron coming before as a guide, and attended by many people. They never came without the father's permission. Entering the chamber, they stood before their father, who ordered them to sit; then the guide spoke and greeted the ruler in the name of all his daughters. Meanwhile they all sat very silently, even the smallest child. The guide gave the father the presents of roses and other flowers and fruit they had brought him, and the embroidery they had woven for him. . . . The father spoke to his daughters, advising them to be good and heed the counsel of their mothers and teachers, to show much respect and obedience for them, and to work carefully. The maidens made no other reply than to approach him one by one and make a low obeisance, after which they departed. None laughed in his presence, but all acted very soberly and modestly.   (Zorita)

They must often have envied plebeian children who spent so much time with their parents and for whom the rules of deportment were far less strict.

Besides the education in the home, there was free schooling for all Mexican children. Some early manuscripts say this began at five years, but the Codex Mendoza states that children up

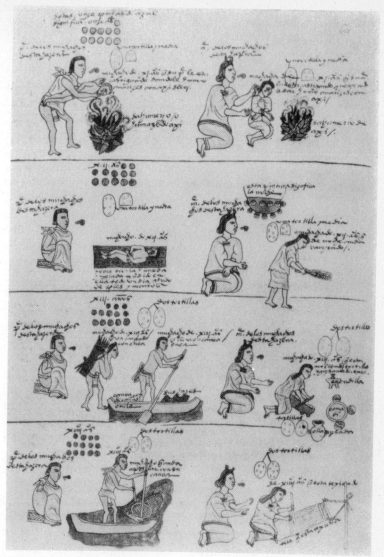

18 The education of children (from the Codex Mendoza). The dots show the ages of the children, and the round objects are the numbers of tortillas they are allowed. In the upper row and second left, disobedient children are punished; elsewhere (left-hand column) fathers teach their sons to carry loads, handle a canoe, and catch fish, while mothers (right-hand column) show their daughters how to sweep the house, grind maize, and weave on a belt loom

to the age of 15 still spent a lot of time at home, although they probably attended school part-time. There were two kinds of school, one (called the *Telpochcalli*, or 'House of Youth') for the sons of tradesmen and peasants, and another (the *Calmecac*) for the sons of the upper classes. All boys were compelled to attend one type of school or the other. Girls of good family were sent away to the temple to be trained as priestesses, although most of them left after a few years when they were asked in marriage. An education of *telpochcalli* type was also available for girls, but each sex had its own school.

Mexican education was above all a training for citizenship. Sahagún's Aztec informants described the ideal schoolboy as 'teachable, tractable, one who can be directed . . . obedient, intelligent, respectful, fearful, one who bows in reverence, obeys, respects others, is indoctrinated'. It is the last word which gives the game away. Nowhere in this list of virtues is there any reference to intellectual curiosity. The idea that knowledge is valuable for its own sake would, if it was ever considered at all, have been dismissed as irrelevant to the needs of Aztec society. Why should the common man learn skills he would never use or, to take the argument one stage further, why should he be taught to think for himself when there were officials to do the job for him?

The whole aim of Mexican education was to teach the child what the state felt he should know, given his social origins and the probable career ahead of him, and to produce what modern jargon would call a 'socially adjusted' individual. Independence and nonconformity were discouraged, and the two-school system, with one type of education for the rich and one for the poor, helped to perpetuate the distinction between the nobility and the lower classes.

Each *calpulli*, or clan (pp. 79–80), maintained a House of Youth where the children of commoners were trained. Usually the school stood close to the clan temple, and it was administered by warriors who had proved their worth by taking several prisoners in battle. Each *telpochcalli* was headed by an elder, the *tlacatecatl* (School Director), who was assisted by a hierarchy of senior and ordinary instructors. There were no fees, and the school was maintained by the revenue from cultivated fields set apart for its support. Although the boys slept at the school they returned home for meals and spent part of each day with their fathers, learning practical skills and the trades they would follow as adults. At harvest time the sons of farmers were allowed a few days' absence to help in the fields, and when they returned they brought back some of the crop they had gathered.

In the House of Youth the boys learned Mexican history and what may loosely be called 'social studies', including religion, ritual, correct behaviour, and music, singing and dancing—the last three not for any artistic or cultural value they might have, but because they played an important part in religious observances. A *telpochcalli* education included none of the traditional 'three Rs' and since there were no schoolbooks the teaching was entirely oral and practical, with a great deal of learning by heart. Slackers were punished by having their heads singed and shaved.

The course was also designed to toughen the boys and to prepare them for the hardships of war. To this end life in the school was deliberately made uncomfortable: the young men received a Spartan training, 'for they ate but a little hard bread, and they slept with little covering and half exposed to the night air in rooms and quarters open like porches' (Zorita). The warrior-teachers showed them how to handle weapons, and the most able boys took part in real battles while the others watched and studied army manœuvres. There was also plenty of hard physical work, sweeping the school and the temple, fetching water and firewood, making adobe bricks, repairing irrigation ditches and canals, or working on the school lands. In the evening they were free to relax. Work finished just before sunset, and the boys went home to bathe and change before returning to the *telpochcalli* where they lit a great fire and danced until midnight when it was time to retire to their quarters.

The *telpochcalli* schools were for the training of ordinary citizens. The *calmecac* schools, on the other hand, were for the education of the élite, the boys from whom future priests, military leaders, judges, and senior administrators would be chosen. The number of places was limited and most of the entrants belonged to the noble classes, but a few tradesmen's children were admitted and even boys of poor plebeian families if they showed unusual intelligence.

The *calmecac* schools were attached to the temples and came under the direct control of the religious authorities. All the instructors were priests (the most highly educated class in ancient Mexico) and the atmosphere was more like that of a monastery than an ordinary school. The boys slept there, and prepared and ate all their meals in the building under the constant supervision of the masters.

The aim of the *calmecac* was to teach 'good habits, doctrine, and exercises'. In addition to the subjects taught in the *telpochcalli*, pupils in the *calmecac* were instructed in medicine, government, mathematics, calendrics and astrology, law, architecture, writing, and religion with all its complicated rituals.

The curriculum laid emphasis on self-control, humility, and unselfishness, for the teachers believed that those who were to lead must first learn to obey. Appropriately enough, the god of the *calmecac* was Quetzalcoatl who was both the symbol of self-abnegation and the patron of knowledge. Although the youths were mostly of high birth they were given menial tasks to do, like cleaning and sweeping, or farm-work on the temple lands, or the collection of firewood in the hills. They were made to fast and to do penance, going alone at night to deserted places in the mountains, sometimes as much as two leagues away from the school, where they offered incense and mortified their flesh by drawing blood from their ears and legs with maguey spines. At midnight, all the boys were roused from their beds to pray and to take a cold bath in the pool.

The *calmecac* schools for girls were equally strict. The buildings were surrounded by high walls, and the teachers were aged priestesses. Whenever the girls went out they were chaperoned by old women, and were forbidden to speak to boys. At meal times no talking was allowed, and during the day there were periods of compulsory silence—the most severe form of discipline which one could inflict on little girls. By day they received instruction in religion and the women's crafts of weaving and embroidery, and at night they had to get up several times in order to pray and offer incense.

Marriage

When a young man reached maturity his parents began to look around for a girl who would make him a suitable wife. Marriage was expected of him but not enforced, although (says Zorita) 'almost none refused to marry when admonished to do so'.

The choice of partner was not left to the young man alone. In theory at least, the whole matter was arranged by the families concerned, and tales of runaway marriages suggest that sometimes parents tried to prevent what they considered unsuitable matches. Astrologers were also called in to study the horoscopes of the couple to make sure that the marriage would turn out well.

Once the relatives of the youth had chosen a bride, they enrolled the services of old women who acted as match-makers and who approached the girl's family on behalf of the prospective bridegroom. The Aztecs were not people to do things simply, and negotiations between the two families had to follow a set routine. The girl's relatives, of course, knew perfectly well what was in the air, but even if they approved of the match custom required them to reject the first overtures. After listening to the visitors they made polite excuses—that their daughter was too young, that really she was unworthy of such a fine young man, that all the members of the family would have to be consulted before any decision could be made, and so on—but they were careful not to make the refusal too final. After a few days, the old women came back again and reopened the matter. With a pretence of reluctance, the girl's parents gave way, and the final discussions were about more practical matters like the size of the bride's dowry and what gifts would be made by the groom's family.

In the meantime, the young man requested formal permission to leave his school. This was never refused, and if a youth was poor he received a gift of produce from the *telpochcalli* storehouse.

In the period of preparation for the wedding the couple had to put up with a lot of well-meant advice from their elders, besides, one suspects, a good deal of teasing which has not been recorded. Fathers addressed their sons in words like these:

Do what pertains to your office. Labour, sow and plant your trees, and live by the sweat of your brow. Do not cast off your burden, or grow faint, or be lazy; for if you are negligent and lazy you will not be able to support yourself or your wife and children.... Love and show charity; be not proud, and do no harm to others; be well bred and civil, and you will be loved and well regarded.... Obey your elders. . . . Do not grumble or answer rudely your parents or those who counsel you to labour.   (Zorita)

65

The same author quotes a sample of a mother's advice to her daughter:

> When your parents give you a husband, do not be disrespectful to him; listen to him and obey him, and do cheerfully what you are told. Do not turn your face from him; and if he did you some hurt, do not keep recalling it. And if he supports himself by your industry, do not on that account scorn him, or be peevish or ungracious, for you will offend God, and your husband will be angry with you. Tell him meekly what you think should be done. Do not insult him or say offensive words to him in front of strangers or even to him alone, for you will harm yourself thereby, and yours will be the fault.

The husband, then, was master of the house, but the woman had a good deal to say about its running and she did not lose her rights as a citizen when she married. She could own property, could make contracts and engage in business, could sue for justice in the courts, and could petition for a divorce if her husband treated her badly. Normally her duties as housewife and mother were enough to occupy her time. A woman was not expected to have a career, but under certain circumstances she could become a professional midwife, match-maker, or healer, though these professions were reserved for old and experienced women.

A 16-year-old girl on the brink of marriage was more concerned with the problems of setting up house than with choosing a career, and as the day for the ceremony drew near the preparations for the wedding took up most of her attention. The bride's family gave the most splendid feast it could afford, inviting friends and relatives, the former schoolmasters of the groom, and all the notabilities of the village or neighbourhood. For two or three days before the banquet the womenfolk busied themselves with preparing tamales and decorating the house with flowers.

At midday the visitors began to arrive with presents for the bride, then everyone sat down to a banquet which followed the usual Aztec pattern with speeches of congratulation from everybody. In the afternoon the bride was adorned for the ceremony. She bathed and washed her hair, made up her face with a yellow cosmetic paste, and covered her arms and legs with red feathers. Dressed in this finery, she sat on a dais by the fire awaiting more callers, this time the elders of the

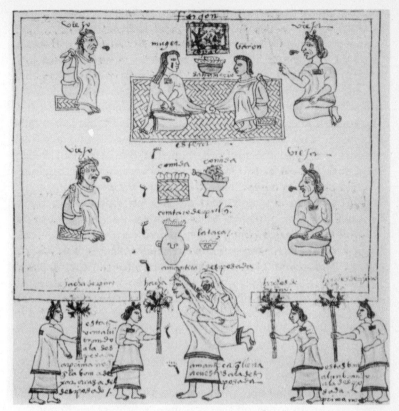

19 The marriage ceremony (Codex Mendoza). Below is the wedding procession, and above is shown the knotting together of garments and the food for the marriage banquet

groom's family who came to welcome her and to wish her happiness.

When it was dark, the marriage procession set out for the bridegroom's house. First walked the relatives of the groom, then came the bride, carried on the back of one of the match-makers, and finally the relations and unmarried friends of the girl, all of them carrying torches of pine wood. Singing songs and shouting good wishes, the procession made its way through the streets to the house where the bridegroom's parents met the girl and conducted her to where the young man was waiting, seated on a mat beside the hearth.

This was where the marriage rite took place. The couple perfumed each other with incense and then sat down on mats placed side by side before the hearth. First they were presented with the traditional gifts; the bridegroom received a loincloth and mantle from the girl's mother, while his own mother offered the bride a blouse and skirt. Finally the couple were quite literally joined together by the match-maker who knotted the young man's cloak to the girl's blouse. They were now man and wife. Two old men and two old women, who acted as witnesses, offered incense and then laid out a feast of turkey stew, toasted maize, and tamales(19). There were further long-winded homilies about how the newly married pair should conduct themselves, and then at last everybody could relax, with singing and dancing, good things to eat, and (for those whose age allowed it) plentiful supplies of *octli*.

The party went on until the younger people ran out of energy and the old ones became completely drunk, but the newly married couple retired early to the bridal chamber to begin a four-day vigil of prayer, leaving the room only at noon and midnight when they offered incense at the family altar. On the fifth day they emerged and cleansed themselves in the steam bath. The union was blessed by a priest who sprinkled the young people with water, and the festivities ended with yet another banquet.

Provided that he was able to support them all, there was no limit to the number of wives a man might take. Economic reasons normally prevented an ordinary man from marrying more than once, but among the noble classes it was usual to introduce secondary wives into the household. Nezahualpilli of Texcoco had more than 2,000 wives and 144 children, if the chronicles can be believed, but this figure seems exceptional even for the ruler of a major state. Montezuma is credited with 19 children, Tezozomoc with 11, and the families of Axayácatl and Ahuítzotl were not much larger. What is certain, however, is that an upper-class Mexican family was usually polygamous, and, among the nobility at least, the secondary wives would require their own quarters, personal servants, and nursemaids.

Among the women one was recognized as the principal wife. She alone was married with the full rites described above, and in the household she took precedence over all the others. If she was the principal wife of a ruler her position was that of an official consort, and the heir to the throne was more likely to be chosen from among her sons. But secondary wives were lawfully married; their sons were recognized as legitimate half-brothers to those of the principal wife, and by virtue of the father's position their children became members of the nobility. A secondary wife had no reason to feel ashamed of her place in the household, and often she was a woman of beauty and intelligence whose humble origins made her unacceptable as a principal wife.

In a country where war and sacrifice took heavy toll of the male population there were obvious advantages in polygamy. It had also its political uses, and the system of secondary wives allowed a ruler to ally himself by marriage with any number of other dynasties. Many such alliances were made for diplomatic reasons rather than for love, and Aztec histories show that the results were not always happy.

The punishment for adultery was death by stoning or strangulation, but an unhappy marriage could be ended by divorce. A man could divorce his wife if she neglected her household jobs, was ill-tempered, or was unable to bear children, but the wife also had her rights and could sue for divorce if the husband beat her, deserted her, or failed to support and educate the children of the marriage. Divorce was not made easy, and the case had to be tried in court where the aim of the judges was to bring about a reconciliation. When the marriage could not be patched up, the court made a settlement of the joint property. If a man was found guilty of abandoning his family, the wife obtained her freedom, was granted custody of the children, and received a half share of all property owned by the couple.

Divorced people were free to remarry and were encouraged to do so. Widows, who must have been fairly numerous in a nation perpetually at war, could also marry again, and a woman whose husband had died was often taken as a secondary wife by one of his brothers—a convenient way of maintaining family solidarity and providing for dependents.

Death

The Aztecs did not fear death, but its existence was never very far from their thoughts. The inevitability of death is a recurrent theme in Nahuatl poetry, and the Mexican attitude is well expressed in a song attributed to the philosopher king, Nezahualcoyotl:

> Even jade will shatter,
> Even gold will crush,
> Even quetzal plumes will tear.
> One does not live forever on this earth:
> Only for an instant do we endure.

And after death—what? The question is asked in another poem:

> Where are we going, ay, where are we going?
> Will we be dead there, or will we live still?
> Will there be existence again there?
> Will we feel again the joy of the Giver of Life?

There can be only one answer, and it is given elsewhere in yet another poem:

> Perchance are we to live a second time?
> Your heart knows it:
> Only once have we come to live.

Death was the extinction of life on earth. All links with those who remained alive were severed, and there was no hope of rebirth.

Except when it came unexpectedly, death was preceded by confession before a priest of the goddess Tlazolteotl, Eater of Filth, the deity who inspired vicious desires in man but who had also the power to forgive sins and to grant absolution. Confession allowed a man to die with a clear conscience, since his sins (including civil crimes as well as transgressions against the moral code) once admitted to a priest could no longer be punished by the law. Absolution, however, was granted only once in a lifetime, and to gain the maximum benefit from it most people put off confession until the last possible moment.

What happened to the soul after death depended not upon conduct during life but on the manner of dying. For the Aztecs the most exalted fate was death in battle or sacrifice. Warriors killed in this manner went straight to the Eastern Paradise (the House of the Sun) where they lived in gardens filled with flowers and passed their time in fighting mock battles. Every morning they assembled on a great open plain, waiting for the sun to rise. When it appeared over the eastern horizon the souls of the warriors greeted it by clashing their swords and lances against their shields, and the whole throng escorted the Sun on the first part of its journey through the sky. Even enemy warriors or sacrificed prisoners could become 'companions of the Sun' on equal terms with Aztecs. After four years, the souls returned to earth in the form of humming-birds or brilliantly coloured butterflies.

Women who died in childbirth were accorded the same esteem as warriors killed in battle. Their souls went to the Western Paradise (the House of Corn) where they turned into the goddesses called *ciuapipiltin*. When the warriors of the Eastern Paradise had carried the Sun on its litter of quetzal plumage as far as the zenith, they relinquished it to the *ciuapipiltin* who accompanied it as far as the western horizon where it disappeared at sunset to pass through the dark regions of the underworld. The souls of these women could return to earth after four years in paradise. Some of them became moths, but other *ciuapipiltin* appeared at night in the form of demons or phantoms which brought disaster to all who saw them. In the manuscripts they are depicted with a skull in place of the head and with claws on their hands and feet.

Warriors were cremated, but women who died in childbirth were buried at sunset in the courtyard of the Temple of the Ciuapipiltin. The corpse was washed, the hair combed out so that it hung loose, and the body dressed in fine garments. Just before sunset the cortège departed for the temple, the husband carrying the body on his shoulders, escorted by midwives and by a crowd of old women bearing swords and shields. This was a necessary precaution, for the body of one of these 'goddess-women' had great powers for good or evil. A lock of hair and a middle finger of the left hand would, if attached to a shield, make a warrior invincible, and as the funerary procession wound through the streets there were sometimes scuffles between the mourners and bands of young men who tried to seize and mutilate the body. Even when the corpse had been buried it was not safe from violation. Body-snatchers came stealthily by night to try and obtain the left arm for use in black magic, and the husband or his friends were forced to keep watch beside the grave until, after four days, the body had lost its potency and could be left in peace.

Tlaloc, the god of rain and water, ruled over Tlalocan, the Southern Paradise. To his domain went the souls of those who had committed suicide, been struck by lightning, had drowned, or died of leprosy, rheumatism, or dropsy, the diseases associated with Tlaloc. The bodies were not cremated but were buried, and on the tomb was laid a dry bough which was supposed to turn green again when the soul arrived in its paradise. Before placing the body in the tomb, relatives smeared liquid rubber on the face of the corpse and decorated its forehead with blue paper. An imitation lock of hair, also made from paper, was attached to the back of the head, then paper capes were wrapped round the shoulders, and wooden staves were placed in each hand.

Tlaloc's paradise was a land of everlasting springtime, where flowers were always in bloom and there was no shortage of things to eat. In a pre-Aztec fresco from Teotihuacán we can see how the souls amused themselves in Tlalocan. Tiny mani-kin-like figures (representing the souls of the dead) wander through a landscape of rivers, mountains, and trees, enjoying themselves in various ways. Some are playing games or swimming in the streams, others picking flowers or chasing butterflies, and from the speech scrolls which issue from their mouths a few of them appear to be singing. Many of the figures carry the green branches mentioned above.

People who died of old age, or from a cause which did not qualify them for admittance to a paradise, went to an underworld called Mictlan (the Place of the Dead) which lay in the far north and was presided over by Mictlantecuhtli, a god who wore a skull mask and whose body was covered with human bones. To get there the soul had to journey through eight hells before arriving at the ninth hell, where Mictlantecuhtli and his consort lived.

Each stage of the journey was beset with difficulties. The soul had first to cross a wide and swift river. For this the aid of a red or yellow dog was needed, and dogs of the correct colour were reared in the household and killed at funerals. In the second hell the soul had to pass between two mountains which clashed together; in the third realm it had to climb a mountain made of obsidian; in the fourth it passed through a region of icy winds which cut like obsidian knives; in the fifth hell the soul entered a place where banners waved; in the sixth arrows were shot at it; in the seventh hell were savage beasts which fed on human hearts; in the eighth the soul had to climb narrow paths between the rocks. Finally, after four years of torment, the dead soul reached the ninth and deepest hell. There at last it found rest and was destroyed for ever.

The bodies of people destined for Mictlan were cremated. Friends and relatives gathered round the deathbed and prayed:

20 Corpse wrapped ready for cremation
(Codex Magliabecchiano)

And now, verily, Mictlantecuhtli receiveth thee . . . for thou hast removed to the abode of the dead, to the place of descent, to the end of journeyings, and to the place of no outlets and no openings. For no more mayest thou make thy return, thy way back. Yea, no more mayest thou bethink thyself of what thou hast left behind thee. (Sahagún)

Old men, whose office it was to prepare the body, began to make the paper objects which would be needed for the funeral. When everything was ready, they poured a libation of water over the head of the corpse, saying as they did so, 'Behold that which thou hast enjoyed, that by which thou hast lived on earth.'

The body was placed in a sitting position with the knees tucked under the chin, then blankets and winding sheet were wrapped round it and secured tightly with cords. Finally, the old men added all that was necessary for the journey to Mictlan. The little dog was killed and laid across the knees of the bundle, and in the mouth of the corpse was placed a piece of jade or other green stone, a symbolic heart with which the soul could placate the ravenous beasts of the seventh hell. Masks, clothing, and perfume were given to the dead person so that he would not arrive at the end of his journey without presents for the lord of the underworld. The corpse was further adorned with insignia made of paper and feathers, and the body of a rich man was hung with jewellery(20).

If it was a king who had died, rulers from all the nearby towns came with offerings and joined a solemn procession made up of relatives, friends, wives of the deceased, and priests who chanted hymns and prayers. The funeral pyre was made ready at the foot of a pyramid, and while the body was being cremated the mourners cast their offerings into the flames. As many as 100 slaves were sacrificed to act as servants on the journey to Mictlan, but their bodies, whether burned or not, were buried separately from that of their master.

The funerary rites of ordinary people followed the same pattern but were on a less elaborate scale. Instead of the multitude of priests, a plebeian corpse was attended by two old men whose job was to press the body back into the flames until it 'cracked and popped', and smelled foul, but even the most humble man was given a bowl of water to sustain him on the journey, and was provided with his shield, his weapons, and with warm clothes to keep out the bitter winds of the fourth hell. On a woman's pyre the relatives laid her weaving materials, baskets, and the clothes she had worn in life.

When the pyre had cooled, the ashes of the deceased were gathered up and placed with a fragment of green stone in a jar or a stone box. This was buried either in the house or in the temple precinct, but rulers were allowed a fine vault lined with masonry and lime plaster.

Offerings of quails and rabbits, tobacco, incense, and flowers or butterflies were left at the burial place after 80 days, and again every year at the Feast of the Dead. When four years had passed, and the soul had found repose in Mictlan, no more offerings were made.

4

Civil Life

During the two centuries which had elapsed since the Aztecs migrated into the Valley of Mexico their social structure had undergone great changes. Their tribal chieftain had been transformed into a semi-divine king, and from the time of Montezuma I (1440–68) the politicians had deliberately encouraged class distinctions. The first clause in Montezuma's law code states quite baldly that 'The king must never appear in public unless the occasion is extremely important', and throughout Mexican society a man's status in the community depended on his rank. There were plenty of offices to be filled, for the growth of Tenochtitlán had been accompanied by the development of a civil service with many grades of official (21). These words of Fray Diego Durán, although written in the sixteenth century about pre-Conquest Mexico, have an all too familiar ring about them:

> The nation had a special official for every activity, small though it were. Everything was so well recorded that no detail was left out of the accounts. There were even officials in charge of sweeping. The good order was such that no one dared to interfere with the job of another or express an opinion since he would be rebuffed immediately. . . . And so the officials of the Republic were innumerable.

The ruling classes

At the apex of the social pyramid was the ruler himself, set apart from the people by his wealth and authority, and separated from them by a barrier of courtly ritual. Even his most important subordinates were kept at a distance, and Bernal Díaz has left this account of the way in which the captains of the royal bodyguard entered the king's presence:

75

They were obliged to take off their rich cloaks and put on others of little value. They had to be clean and to enter barefoot, with their eyes downcast, for they were not allowed to look him in the face. And they had to make him three obeisances, saying as they came towards him, 'Lord, my Lord, my great Lord!' Then when they had made their report, he would dismiss them with a few words. They did not turn their backs as they went out, but kept their faces towards him and their eyes to the ground, turning round only when they had left the room.

When the king travelled, his litter was carried on the shoulders of noblemen.

The ruler of Tenochtitlán was commander-in-chief of the armies of the Triple Alliance, and also held the title of *tlatoani* (He who Speaks). The Aztecs followed the custom of most of the Valley tribes in choosing their king by election, but from the time of Acamapichtli, first lord of Tenochtitlán, the ruler had always been chosen from a single family, though not always in the most direct line of descent.

In the days when the Aztecs were a small tribe it had been easy to test public opinion by consulting the heads of families, but by the sixteenth century this method had become too unwieldy and the electoral body had shrunk to about 100 people, drawn from the ranks of the nobility and the more important officials, priests, and warriors. No vote was taken, but the electors conferred among themselves and decided on an acceptable candidate who was then presented to the people to be approved by acclamation. There are no records of a refusal to accept the council's nominee. As a courtesy to the other rulers of the Alliance, the kings of Texcoco and Tlacopan were asked to confirm the appointment, and at the election of Tizoc in 1481 it was the lord of Texcoco who placed the turquoise diadem on the new ruler's head.

Election depended on merit, and the job of the council was to choose the most able person among the male relatives of the deceased ruler. The electors looked for a man who had proved his valour in battle, had a good record of public service, and was prudent and just in his conduct. In a polygamous society there was no lack of candidates, for a ruler normally had sons by several of his wives—not to mention the host of brothers, half-brothers, uncles, cousins, and other relatives who were also eligible for selection.

21 Montezuma's palace in Tenochtitlán (Codex Mendoza). On the upper terrace the ruler sits in his throne-room which is flanked by guest-rooms for allied chiefs. On the ground floor is the meeting-room of the war council (left) and of the judges and councillors (right)

Sometimes the choice fell on a son of the previous ruler. In theory the throne was offered to the most deserving candidate, but in practice there were all sorts of political factors to be considered. Powerful connections were always a help, and Chimalpopoca was elected ruler at the age of 10 or 11 largely because his mother was a daughter of Tezozomoc, lord of Azcapotzalco, to whom the Aztecs were paying tribute at the time. In the later period, when the Aztecs were the dominant power in Mexico, dynastic alliances became less important to them and the council elected a series of vigorous and successful men.

Often the throne was occupied by several brothers in succession. On the death of Axayácatl in 1481 the office descended

77

first to his brother Tizoc, and then to another brother, Ahuítzotl, before the direct line resumed in the person of Axayácatl's son, Montezuma II.

The ruler was assisted by a dignitary known as Ciuacoatl (Snake Woman), who, despite this title, was a man, and who dealt with mundane affairs of government. He was president of the high court, served as deputy ruler in the king's absence, and acted as chairman of the electoral college whenever a king died. Below the Snake Woman in the hierarchy came the military commanders of the four wards into which Tenochtitlán was divided, and below them again the city council, which in theory had the right to make policy decisions although in practice it always bowed to the wishes of the ruler. In older and more democratic days the council members seem to have been the elected delegates of the clans, but by the time of the Conquest most councillors were nominated by the ruler.

The class which can be roughly translated as the 'nobility' was made up of high officials who included senior generals, heads of the various branches of the civil service, judges of the appeal court, rulers of conquered cities, governors of provincial towns and of the districts of Tenochtitlán. These men were lords by virtue of the offices they held, and not through birth or inheritance like the traditional European aristocracy. They may perhaps be compared with the Life Peers of the House of Lords. A *tecuhtli* paid no taxes, was given an official residence, and drew his income from lands pertaining to his office rather than his person. During his lifetime he bore all the insignia of his rank, and in conversation the ending *tzin* was added to his name as a mark of respect, in much the same way as we use expressions like 'Sir' or 'Your Worship'.

Unlike a hereditary lord, however, a *tecuhtli* could not be sure that his son would take over the office and all the benefits which went with it. The private family estates could indeed be passed down from father to son, but the public lands remained tied to the particular office and reverted to the king when an official died or retired. If there was a suitably qualified male relative in the family the job usually went to him, but the final decision lay with the ruler who could appoint anyone he thought fit.

Sons of *tecuhtli* belonged by right of birth to the lesser nobility, the *pilli*. Their aristocratic background and education gave them certain advantages (and it was among them that the ruler

78

chose many of his officials), but wealth and prestige came from rank rather than birth, and a *pilli* was expected to work as hard as anybody else. The frontier between the common people and the ruling class was easily crossed in both directions. A plebeian who distinguished himself by taking four captives in battle was given official rank and could aspire to high position; on the other hand, a *pilli* was expected to make his own way in the world, and if he did nothing outstanding in his lifetime he was not promoted to any official position and in consequence left his children neither honour nor wealth.

The common people

Below the nobles and civil servants came the mass of the people, the free commoners, organized into *calpulli*, or hereditary clans. All members of a clan considered themselves related by descent from a common ancestor, usually a figure said to have lived at the time when the land was first occupied and divided among the people, and by the time of the Conquest there were 20 such clans in Tenochtitlán proper, plus those of Tlatelolco which was annexed in 1473.

The original clans may well have been kinship groups, but during two centuries of urban life the bonds of kinship had become less important than those of residence. The word *calpulli* means 'group of houses', and in the sixteenth century the clans were primarily landholding corporations each of which occupied its own ward of the city and also owned farmland which it distributed among clan members, allotting each family enough for its needs. Within the *calpulli*, families were grouped into units of 20 which were combined into major units of 100 households.

Superimposed on the clan system was a division of the city for administrative purposes into four great sectors. Each of these quarters housed several *calpulli* and was governed by a military chief who was appointed by the central authority and was generally a member of the royal family.

The *calpulli* were in many ways like modern parishes. Each clan maintained its own temple and school, and local affairs were dealt with by a council of clan elders which copied in miniature the structure of the central government. The head of the *calpulli* was elected by the members of the clan and held office for life. It was his responsibility to distribute land, to make sure that the registers were kept up to date, to represent the clan in lawsuits, to pass on the commands of officials higher up the ladder, and to oversee the work of the minor clan officers who each looked after the labour and taxation of a few households.

The head of the clan was also president of the local council and had the dubious privilege of paying for the food and drink consumed at meetings. Since he was also responsible for entertaining visitors the expenses of his office could be high, but in compensation he paid no taxes and drew an income from lands tilled by his fellow clansmen. In more ancient times the head of a *calpulli* had been a powerful man, but under a centralized government he had become a minor cog in the administrative machine. Important matters were decided at city level, and only the most petty local business was entrusted to clan officials.

Two sections of the community, the *mayeques* and the slaves, were outside the clan structure altogether. The *mayeques*, who numbered about 30 per cent of the total population, were free men who belonged to the depressed class of landless peasants. Because they were not members of any clan they received no share in the distribution of farmland and gained no benefit from the welfare services of the *calpulli*. They were not slaves, nor were they full citizens. The origins of the *mayeque* class are obscure, but since every Aztec born of free parents was automatically a member of his ancestral clan we must assume that many *mayeques* were of non-Aztec stock, perhaps newcomers to the Valley, or the descendants of conquered tribes. Others were free commoners who had lost their civil rights through debt or crime, and still others were the children of slaves who were born free but who inherited no clan rights.

The slaves

A *mayeque*, however miserable his condition, was at least a free man. A slave, on the other hand, was owned outright by his master and could be put to any kind of work at his master's pleasure. Female slaves were given jobs in the kitchens and in workshops where they wove cloth or made garments; males worked in the fields, acted as house-servants, porters, and labourers. Although a slave received no pay, his lot was in many ways more comfortable than that of a landless peasant. We never hear of a prosperous *mayeque*, but a slave could always be

sure of food and shelter, and—unlike a free man—escaped the
twin burdens of military service and taxation. Many slaves rose
to positions of responsibility, acting as overseers or estate
managers, and Aztec law allowed them to acquire land, property, and even slaves of their own. There are many cases of a
widow marrying one of her slaves, and it was not uncommon for
a man to take a slave girl as a concubine. There was nothing
shameful in such a union, and Itzcoatl, one of the greatest
rulers of Tenochtitlán, was elected king even though his mother
was a slave, and his father, Acamapichtli, had other sons by a
noblewoman of the Colhuacán dynasty.

The principal slave market was in Azcapotzalco where the
trade was so well organized that the dealers were among the
richest of the merchants. Each dealer owned three or four
buildings in the city, and there he housed his slaves until the day
came to parade them, dressed in borrowed finery, before the
crowd of buyers in the market square. Singers and drummers
were hired for the occasion, and the slaves were made to display
their skills in dancing and music. An ordinary slave with no
special skills cost about 20 cotton mantles (no mean price, for a
poor man could live for almost a year on that sum), but a good
dancer could fetch 30 or even 40 mantles. When the bargaining
was over, the dealer stripped off all the fine clothes and the
purchaser replaced them with everyday wear before sending the
slave to a wooden cage (23) where he waited until his new owner
collected him.

Most of the slaves who reached the markets had come from
distant lands, often outside Aztec territory. As part of their
tribute some of the border cities were required to send slaves to
Mexico, a demand which they satisfied by raiding their neighbours, the Tarascans, Mixtecs, Tlappanecs, and other tribes
not subject to the Alliance. Other slaves were purchased by
merchants in Tehuantepec or the towns of the Gulf Coast, and
the laws make it clear that stealing children for sale to slave-
dealers was a profitable crime in the Aztec homeland as well as
abroad.

A slave who got as far as the market had one last chance of
regaining his freedom. If he could escape from the market place
and reach the sanctuary of the ruler's palace he became a free
man, and the law gave him a sporting chance by forbidding
anybody except the owner or the owner's son to try and catch

him. Any other person who interfered in the chase was punished by being enslaved himself.

Some slaves were criminals sentenced for theft or non-payment of debts. Others were voluntary slaves who had sold themselves in return for shelter and security. In this latter group were peasants whose crops had failed or who were unable to pay their taxes, but also less deserving characters, such as gamblers and drunkards, who were either too lazy to till their own fields or else had ruined themselves by extravagance. For all these people there was hope. Thieves were freed when they had repaid the value of the stolen goods, and any slave could buy his liberty by paying his master a sum equivalent to his purchase price. Often, too, slaves were freed when their master died.

In another form of voluntary slavery the contract was for the service itself rather than for the labour of one particular individual. In exchange for a loan a poor man might offer one of his sons as a slave, or a group of families might combine to promise a fixed amount of work in the fields or to offer one of their members as a household slave. Provided that these services were properly carried out it made little difference who actually did the job, and it often happened that after a few years of slavery the bondsman was replaced by a younger relative who served for a few years before handing over to somebody else in his turn. The children of slaves were free, and Aztec society had no class of hereditary serfs.

Even in the sixteenth century, when Aztec power was at its height, slaves were not numerous (perhaps about two per cent of the total population) and we are still a long way from the dependence on slave labour which characterized so many ancient civilizations of the Old World.

A Mexican slave, although he was his master's chattel, still kept a certain dignity as a person. The Aztec attitude may be summed up in the phrase, 'There, but for the grace of God, go I', and the fortunate man tended to regard a slave as somebody who had been born under an unlucky sign and whose misfortune was caused as much by fate as by weakness. Slaves were an expensive investment, and even the Spanish chroniclers agree that they were well treated by their owners.

The sale of slaves was governed by law. A well-behaved slave could not be sold without his consent, but custom allowed a master to get rid of a slave who was dishonest, lazy, or disobedient. A heavy wooden collar was placed around the man's neck (22) and he was put up for sale again in the market. If this lesson did not teach him to mend his ways an even greater danger awaited him. An incorrigible slave, who had had three owners and failed to satisfy any of them, forfeited all sympathy and could now be bought for sacrifice.

22 Slaves (Codex Florentino)

Law and justice

Every aspect of a citizen's life was regulated by law. Legislation covered civil matters such as property rights, debts, contracts, and divorce, while other branches of the law dealt with criminal offences (theft, assault, treason, etc.) and with such matters as public drunkenness or insulting the ruler's dignity.

Petty crimes were dealt with by the local courts which met in the smaller towns and in each district of the big cities. In these lesser courts the judges were commoners, experienced warriors and people of 'sound and righteous upbringing', but their jurisdiction was limited to minor offences. In the case of more serious crime the local court arrested the delinquent and carried out a preliminary examination before handing the matter on to a more senior court, the Teccali, which met in Tenochtitlán and in each provincial capital. The Teccali court, with a president and two assistant judges, was permanently in session, and one of its main duties was to pass sentence on cases handed up from the local courts.

The more complicated cases, and all those in which noblemen were involved, were taken to a still higher level and were heard before an Appeal Court presided over by the *Cihuacoatl* (the second highest official of the realm) assisted by judges drawn from the ranks of the aristocracy. This court sat in the ruler's palace, and for all routine affairs was the highest tribunal in the land. One further appeal was possible—to the ruler himself who held court in person every 10 or 12 days and was assisted by judges of the highest rank (21). Most of the early chronicles give the number of these advisers as 12 or 13, but only two are mentioned in Bernal Díaz's account of one of these sessions:

> When an important chief came to discuss a boundary dispute, he brought with him a drawing or painting upon maguey cloth, representing the suit or difficulty about which he had come, and pointed out the grounds for his claim with some thin polished sticks. Beside Montezuma stood two old men, who were great chiefs: and when they thoroughly understood the suit, these judges told Montezuma the rights of the case, which he then settled in a few words. . . .

The proceedings of the courts were carefully recorded by scribes.

The judges were paid a salary from the revenue of lands set aside for the purpose, and were forbidden to accept any other gifts or payment. Any judge who took bribes or was negligent in his duties was removed from office, and for serious misconduct had his house knocked down and all his possessions confiscated. Officials were expected to be incorruptible and fair to everyone, rich or poor, and Nezahualpilli of Texcoco had one of his judges hanged for showing undue favour to a nobleman at the expense of a plebeian.

The court assembled at daybreak, and the judges settled down to hear evidence and examine witnesses. No torture was used to extract confessions—in this respect the Indians appear in a better light than their European conquerors—and witnesses swore in the name of Huitzilopochtli that they would tell the truth. Lying thus became a crime against the gods, and perjury was punished with death. The court sat until midday when the judges' meals were brought from the palace kitchens, then, after only a short rest, business continued until two hours before sundown.

Every 80 days another tribunal met in Tenochtitlán and was attended by representatives from all the provincial capitals. At this meeting each provincial judge gave an account of the cases tried in his area, and any difficult suits were brought up for discussion. This court acted as a Council of State and was allowed to debate matters which concerned the Mexican empire as a whole.

Texcoco was the greatest centre of learning in the Valley of Mexico, and one of its rulers, the famous Nezahualcoyotl, drew up a code of law which was copied, with some local modifications, in Tenochtitlán and Tlacopan as well. The king's aim

23 Prisoners on public display. They are kept in a wooden cage with the roof weighted down by stones
(Codex Florentino)

was to combine sternness with justice, and we can best appreciate his intentions by examining the changes which he made in the old law inherited from his Chichimec ancestors.

The Chichimec Code prescribed death as the punishment for crop-stealing, but Nezahualcoyotl decreed that corn, squashes, and beans should be planted along the edges of roads and ponds for the use of any person in need. Thus poor folk were helped, while those who stole out of greed rather than necessity still paid the full penalty. The harsh forest laws were modified so as to allow country people to collect dead branches for firewood, but in order to preserve the forests the death penalty was retained for any person who cut down a living tree. Death was the punishment for anyone who moved a field boundary.

The law was also used to protect the class structure of Aztec society, and among the statutes of Montezuma I, who lived at the same time as Nezahualcoyotl, are items like these:

> Only the king and the Prime Minister Tlacaelel may wear sandals within the palace. No great chieftain may enter the palace shod, under pain of death. The great noblemen are the only ones to be allowed to wear sandals in the city and no one else, with the exception of men who have performed some great deed in war. But these sandals must be cheap and common; the gilded, painted ones are to be used only by noblemen. . . .
>
> The common people will not be allowed to wear cotton clothing under pain of death, but only garments of maguey fibre. The mantle must not be worn below the knee, and if anyone allows it to reach the ankle, he will be killed, unless he has wounds of war on his legs. . . .

And so the list goes on. Tacked to the end of it, almost as an afterthought, are laws concerning education, adultery, and theft.

No case was allowed to drag on for more than 80 days. Prisoners awaiting trial or execution were kept in wooden cages (23), but long-term imprisonment did not figure in the penal code. Major crimes (which could include adultery, impersonating an official, and being found drunk in public, as well as the more serious offences of highway robbery, witchcraft, treason, and stealing from the market) were punished with death by stoning, strangulation (24), or sacrifice.

For other categories of offence the punishment was based on the principle of restitution to the injured party. A man who assaulted another had to pay the costs of curing the victim and of replacing anything damaged during the brawl. The Texcocan law on canoe-stealing decreed that the thief must pay the owner the value of the canoe, and if this repayment was not made the criminal was enslaved. The same principle applied in Tenochtitlán to all kinds of crime against property. Provided he was over the age of 10 at the time of the offence, any person who stole from a temple, palace, or private house became a slave in the place where the crime was committed until he had repaid the loss twice over, once to the victim and once to the treasury as a fine. Slavery was also the punishment for kidnappers, relatives of traitors, and people who sold goods which were not their own property.

24 Executing a criminal by strangulation
(Codex Florentino)

Noblemen and public servants were expected to set a high standard of conduct. A plebeian who robbed his father was sold into slavery, but for the same crime a nobleman was killed. A drunken official or priest was executed, but if the offender was a common man he got away more lightly. On the first occasion his head was shaved in public and his house knocked down, but if he were unlucky enough to be caught a second time the penalty was death. Even the ruler's family was bound by the law, and Nezahualcoyotl had three of his sons executed for violating the code he had drawn up.

25 Wheeled toy made of red pottery, from a town in Tlaxcala. Probably pre-Aztec

Transport and communications

The Mexicans understood the principle of the wheel, but never applied it to anything bigger than children's pull-along toys in the form of wheeled animals (25). The reason is probably not lack of inventiveness, but rather the absence of suitable draught animals and the ruggedness of the terrain.

In the cities there were paved streets and ceremonial avenues, but the cross-country roads used by messengers and trading caravans were unsurfaced tracks. Some maintenance work was carried out; in jungle country the roads were kept free of vegetation, and everywhere the surfaces were repaired after the rains. Fallen trees were removed, pot-holes filled in, and steps cut on the steeper sections. Canoes or wooden bridges were provided at river crossings, and for the convenience of travellers there were rest houses along the route and shrines where the devout could make offerings.

Within the Valley of Mexico was a network of roads joining the principal towns. One of the most important long-distance roads (which the Spaniards followed, with much suffering, on their march to Tenochtitlán) came up from Xicalango and the trading cities of the Gulf Coast, and further south another road crossed the isthmus of Tehuantepec. In western Mexico was a trade route which linked Tenochtitlán with the Pacific, passing through the country of the Zapotecs in Oaxaca, and terminating on the coast at Huatulco, just south of Acapulco.

In early Colonial times this road was provided with rest houses, and each village along the route was responsible for the upkeep of 20 miles of roadway. It is likely that the Spaniards took over the system of tribute-labour already in force before their arrival, and the Aztec arrangement was probably much the same.

There were no pack animals and no carts; everything had to be transported on the backs of men. Most people carried their own personal equipment, but men of low class sometimes hired themselves out as porters for others. The usual load was between 50 and 60 lb., and the daily journey about 15 miles, though in an emergency the bearers were capable of much more. The load was attached to a carrying-frame made of two stout upright poles, about a body's width apart, with horizontal crosspieces lashed on at intervals. The weight of the burden was taken by a plaited 'tump line' which passed across the porter's forehead, and the frame could be propped up while the carrier rested (26).

At certain periods of the year the roads were especially busy. Tribute of foodstuffs was collected every harvest time from the central provinces of the Empire, and caravans of porters were needed to carry the produce to the capital. A single *troje* of maize (about 200 tons) would make 8,000 individual loads weighing 50 lb. each—and in tribute alone Tenochtitlán received 146 *trojes* of staple foods (maize, beans, sage, and amaranth) every year, not to speak of the firewood, cotton, and other bulky goods. Besides this annual collection there were deliveries of some commodities at half-yearly and 80-day intervals, all of which were additional to troop movements and normal commercial traffic.

Official letters, written on cloth or paper, were tucked into the ends of forked sticks which were carried by relays of runners, and there are tales that the messengers could cover 300 miles in

26 A travelling merchant and his porters halting by the roadside

27 The god, Xochipilli, carried on a litter and preceded by a
herald who blows a conch-shell trumpet (Codex Magliabecchiano)

a single day, a rate of about 12½ miles per hour. Theoretically
this is possible if the messengers worked day and night,
and if each man was a trained runner who covered only
a short distance, but in Peru under the Incas (for which good
figures are available) the daily stint was only 150 miles. This is a
more credible figure for Mexico too, but even at the reduced
rate it is no wonder that Montezuma was kept informed of
every move the Spaniards made, or that the royal table was
supplied with fish brought fresh from the coasts.

The common people walked everywhere, but on state
occasions the nobility were carried in litters, hammocks, or even
on the backs of servants, although these exotic modes of transport were used only for short journeys when it was important to
give an impression of grandeur. The ruler of Texcoco, Díaz
observed, came out to welcome Cortés, 'carried on a litter,
richly worked in green feathers with much silver decoration and
with precious stones set in tree patterns that were worked in
finest gold. His litter was carried on the shoulders of eight chief-
tains, each of whom, it was said, was the ruler of a town.' It is

not surprising that when the gods were carried in procession, they too were borne on litters (27).

The Aztecs had no navy. Sea trade was left in the hands of the coastal tribes, but canoe transport was vital to the lakeside towns in the Valley of Mexico, especially to the island city of Tenochtitlán. On these inland waters canoes carried goods to and from the city, removed waste, ferried warriors and raiding parties, and (like the motor boats on Venetian canals) did many of the jobs carried out by present-day buses and carts. A canoe route connected lakes Zumpango and Xaltocan with the capital, and a southern extension led to the cities of Xochimilco and Chalco. Where necessary, canals 15 to 40 feet wide were cut through the reed beds and kept open by communal labour.

The illustrations in the codices usually depict dugout canoes with upturned ends. These were either poled or paddled, and the drawings usually show a single paddler standing up near the stern. The normal all-purpose canoe was about 14 feet long, but size was limited only by the length of tree trunk available and war canoes were much larger, as was the royal barge which was provided with a throne, an awning, and space for several paddlers. In early Conquest years the largest canoes, made of straight-grained spruce, measured upwards of 50 feet and could carry either 60 passengers or three tons of maize.

Books, documents, and writing

The administration of Tenochtitlán and its foreign provinces required a great deal of paperwork. Taxes had to be collected, lawsuits between villages or private individuals had all to be recorded, and the merchants kept accounts of their goods and profits. Instructions and reports passed to and fro between the capital and the outlying cities, and—like any civilized people of today—the Mexicans were familiar with both red tape and official correspondence. The clans maintained land registers, and when Cortés reached Tenochtitlán he had no trouble in procuring from the royal archive a map showing all the rivers and bays along a 400-mile stretch of the north coast. In addition each temple owned a library of religious and astrological works, while a large private household, like that of Montezuma, employed a full-time steward to look after the accounts which were so many that they filled an entire house.

28 A Mexican screen-fold book (Codex Fejervary Mayer). The bar-and-dot numerals suggest that the workmanship is not Aztec

Ixtlilxochitl, a brother of the last native ruler of Texcoco, has left this account in the prologue to his *Historia Chichimeca:*

They had scribes for each branch of knowledge. Some dealt with the annals, putting down in order the things which happened each year, giving the day, month, and hour. Others had charge of the genealogies, recording the lineage of rulers, lords and noblemen, registering the newborn and deleting those who had died. Some painted the frontiers, limits, and boundary markers of the cities, provinces and villages, and also the distribution of fields, whose they were and to whom they belonged. Other scribes kept the law books and those dealing with the rites and ceremonies which they practised when they were infidels. The priests recorded all matters to do with the temples and images, with their idolatrous doctrines, the festivals of their false gods, and their calendars. And finally, the philosophers and learned men which there were among them were charged with painting all the sciences which they had discovered, and with teaching by memory all the songs in which were embodied their scientific knowledge and historical traditions.

In the law courts, especially those dealing with land and property rights, the disputants supported their claims with genealogies and maps, showing the king's land in purple, the lords' in red, and the clan fields in yellow.

Of this mass of paperwork hardly anything remains, and nearly all the surviving books from the Aztec homeland are of post-Conquest date. Some are copies of earlier works, while others are written in Aztec script with Spanish or Nahuatl commentaries in European letters. The best collection of pre-Conquest books comes from Oaxaca, the land of the Mixtecs, where more than a dozen examples have been preserved.

Each book, or *codex*, consists of a strip, anything up to 13 yards in length and some 6–7 inches high, made of paper, maguey cloth, or deer skin, and folded in zigzag or concertina fashion like a modern map, so that wherever the user opened it he was confronted by two pages (28). The ends of the strip were glued to thin plaques of wood which served as covers and were sometimes decorated with paintings or with discs of turquoise. Both sides of the strip were covered with writing and pictures, and the individual pages were divided into sections by red or black lines. Each page was normally read from top to bottom, though in some codices the arrangement is zigzag or even goes around the page. The strip was scanned from left to right.

This enormous production of documents was dependent on a steady supply of the raw materials, and each year 24,000 reams of paper, the equivalent of 480,000 sheets, were sent to Tenochtitlán. Aztec paper was made from the inner bark of various species of fig tree. The bark was soaked in a river or in a bath of

limey water, and the fibres were separated from the pulp, then laid on a smooth surface, doubled over, and beaten with a mashing stone which had a ridged surface (29). A binding material (probably a gum of vegetable origin), was added, and the fibres were beaten out into a thin, homogeneous sheet. After smoothing and drying, the processed bark fibres had recognizably become paper,

29 Bark-beater used in the manufacture of paper. The mashing-stone is enclosed in a handle made from a supple twig

but the surfaces were still porous and rough, unsuitable for painting until they had been given a coating of white chalky varnish or size.

On this background the scribe drew his figures, first sketching the outlines in black, then adding the colours with his brush. The principal colours were red, blue, green, and yellow, and the pigments were sometimes mixed with an oil to give added lustre. Scribes were respected craftsmen, and the profession was probably hereditary.

Aztec writing suffered from one great disadvantage: it was non-alphabetic. In an alphabetic script like our own, each letter represents one of the basic sounds of the language, and each word (which is itself a combination of sounds) can be turned into a combination of letters. The advantage of an alphabet is that the whole range of language can be precisely expressed by means of a few symbols which are easy to learn and convenient to write. The Aztecs, however, wrote a form of hieroglyphic script in which all the symbols were pictures of one kind or another.

Many of these pictures (or *glyphs*) were simply *pictograms* in which an object was represented by a miniature drawing of itself, often very much stylized(30 upper). This system is only satisfactory when dealing with objects which can be easily recognized from pictures. It is a simple matter to compile a list of the articles sent to the royal treasury(4), but the method breaks down when required to express abstract ideas or relationships. To some extent the difficulty can be overcome by using the symbols not as pictograms but as *ideograms* in which the objects express not only their own natures but also the underlying ideas and concepts associated with them. Thus the idea of death can be represented by a corpse wrapped for burial, night by a black sky and a closed eye(79), war by a shield and a club, or speech by a little scroll issuing from the mouth of the person who is talking(68). Concepts involving the idea of motion, walking, migration, or the sequence of events were usually indicated by a trail of footprints going in the necessary direction(2).

Aztec personal names were of the descriptive type which could usually be written in glyphs. The name of the Emperor Acamapichtli means 'Handful of Reeds' and his glyph is a forearm with the hand grasping a bundle of stalks. Chimalpopoca, the name of the next ruler but one, means 'Smoking Shield', and his successor was Itzcoatl or 'Obsidian Snake'.

There was also a phonetic element in Aztec writing. Every word in spoken language has a sound as well as a meaning, and glyphs were sometimes used to indicate the phonetic value of a word rather than its sense. Thus, to give an example from English, a drawing of an eye may be a *pictogram* (meaning the eye as part of the body), or an *ideogram* (expressing the idea of sight and vision), or a *phonogram* (standing for the sound 'I'). In the latter case, the eye symbol can be used, as a sort of pun, to indicate the first person singular. It is possible, though clumsy, to write the sentence, 'I can be hospitable', as a series of phonetic glyphs: an eye, a tin can, a bee, a horse, a pit or hole, and a table, but the sounds are only approximate and give no more than a rough guide to pronunciation.

The Aztecs applied the same technique to the writing of Nahuatl(30). Pictures were sometimes used for their sound, without reference to their meaning. The symbol for teeth (*tlantli* in the Aztec language) expressed the syllable 'tlan'; the glyph for tree or forest (*quauitl*) stood for the syllable 'quauh', a stone (*tetl*) for 'te', a mountain (*tepetl*) for 'tepe', and so on. Vowels were sometimes represented phonetically; the sound 'a' by the symbol for water (*atl*), or 'o' by a road (*otli*).

Names of towns could be expressed by a combination of such phonograms. The sign for the Aztec capital, Tenoch-titlán, was a stone (*tetl*) from which sprouted a prickly pear cactus (*nochtli*); Tochtepecan was indicated by a rabbit (*tochtli*) above a mountain (*tepetl*); Quauhtitlan by a tree (*quauitl*) with teeth (*tlantli*), Quauhnauac by a tree with a speech scroll issuing from it (*nahuatl*=speech)(30 lower).

These symbols were not placed in sequence, one after the other like the letters and words in a book, but formed part of a larger composition which often took the form of a scene in which many things may be happening at once. An Aztec manuscript is not *read* in the normal sense of the word, but is *deciphered* like a puzzle picture in which the glyphs provide labels and clues to what is going on.

The lower part of the picture generally represents the ground, while the upper is the sky. Since the Aztecs had not discovered the rules of perspective, distance is shown by placing the furthest figures at the top of the page and the nearest at the bottom.

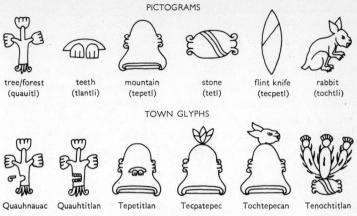

30 Aztec writing. Formation of town glyphs from pairs
of pictograms

Relative importance is indicated by size: a victorious king, for
example, may be drawn larger than his defeated enemy. All
figures are in profile, with no three-quarter views or fore-
shortening.

Every item in a composition is there to give information,
either directly or by implication, and the painter assumes that
the person examining the document is familiar with the insignia
of rank, the costumes appropriate to the various classes, and the
iconography of the different gods. A priest, for instance, is
always depicted with his face painted black, his hair long, and
his ear-lobe stained red from blood-letting. He can thus be
recognized as a priest even when dressed in warrior's costume or
plain garb. In the same way, an old person can be recognized
by the lines which represent the wrinkles on his face (19).

Colour was also important. The signs for grass, canes, and
rushes look very much the same in black and white, but in colour
there could be no mistake: in the Codex Mendoza grass is
yellow, canes are blue, rushes green. A ruler could be recognized
at once from the shape of his diadem and from its colour, turquoise, which was reserved for royal use.

A script of this kind is not a very flexible tool. The information
it can give is only approximate, and the process of writing is
both slow and cumbersome. A scribe who could keep pace with
court proceedings had every reason to be proud of his skill.
Aztec picture-writing gives only the outline of an event or

situation, serving as a kind of aide-memoire to an experienced reader who could fill in the details and background from the material learned by heart in the *calmecac* schools.

Both writing and reading were therefore specialized skills, and it is no wonder that the mass of the population remained illiterate. Writing was not taught in the schools attended by plebeian children, and indeed the ordinary man would have no need for it. In a bureaucratic and centralized society the common man received his instructions from above, from the priests who looked after the religious side of his life, or from the secular officials who were drawn from the nobility and had the benefit of a *calmecac* education.

Counting

The Aztecs used a vigesimal system, counting by 20s. The numbers 1–19 were expressed by dots or occasionally by fingers; 20 was represented by a flag; 400 (i.e. 20 × 20) by a sign which looks like a feather or a fir tree; and 8,000 (20 × 20 × 20) by a bag or tasselled pouch which was imagined to contain 8,000 cocoa beans (4).

5

City Life

Mexico, like ancient Greece or Renaissance Italy, was a country in which the highest political unit was the autonomous city state. The city was not just a collection of buildings or a place to live in, but was a focus for national loyalty, and the embodiment of the hopes and aspirations of its people. Military power, splendid buildings, wealth, fine craftsmanship, intellectual or artistic pre-eminence were the means by which this civic pride was expressed, and the aim of each city was to outshine its rivals.

At the time of the Conquest there were cities and towns clustered all round the shores of the lake which filled the Valley of Mexico(1), but Spanish destruction and modern urban development have between them obliterated almost everything. Archaeology by itself cannot bring Tlatelolco or Tenochtitlán back to life, but through the writings of the Conquistadores we can still feel what it was like to walk through the streets of Montezuma's capital (Frontispiece).

Tenochtitlán

Tenochtitlán in 1519 showed little trace of its origin as a collection of squalid huts built on an island set among swamps and reed beds. By the time of the Conquest, land-reclamation had increased the size of the original island so that it now formed a square with sides about two miles long. Much of this reclaimed ground was liable to subsidence, and wooden piles were driven into the earth to stabilize the foundations of all important or heavy buildings. Excavations carried out in the area behind the cathedral in 1900 revealed thousands of these stakes, and also parts of earthenware water-pipes some 15 feet below the modern surface.

On the north side Tenochtitlán was joined to the island of Tlatelolco, which had been a city in its own right until the war of 1473. After the defeat of the Tlatelolcans, the swamps which separated the islands were drained and the two cities became a single conurbation, although each of the old units kept its own commercial and religious centre. The Aztec capital, with a population of more than 150,000, was the largest city in Mexico and was bigger by far than any European city of the time.

Tenochtitlán-Tlatelolco was linked to the mainland by three raised causeways, each wide enough to allow ten horsemen to ride abreast(1). Two aqueducts brought fresh water into the city. A double pipeline (so constructed that one conduit could remain in use while the other was closed for cleaning and repair) led to the spring at Chapultepec and followed the line of the western causeway, while a second aqueduct brought water along the causeway from Coyoacan to the southern edge of the city from which it ran in a covered channel to the Temple Precinct.

Here and there gaps were left in the causeways to allow canoes to pass from one part of the lake to another, and these canals were spanned by wooden bridges which could be removed at the approach of an enemy. At intervals the aqueducts opened out into reservoirs where men were stationed to fill the canoes of the water-sellers who circulated in every quarter of the city.

To the east stretched open water, and on a clear day the pyramids of Texcoco were just visible on the horizon. Between the two cities was a dyke which Nezahualcoyotl built as a gift for Montezuma I. This dyke was 10 miles long and was provided with sluice gates to control the lake level in times of flood, but its main purpose was to prevent the salt waters of the eastern part of Lake Texcoco from polluting the irrigated gardens of Tenochtitlán. Sealed off behind its dyke, the Aztec capital, like a Mexican Venice, stood in an artificial lagoon fed by fresh-water springs.

Some of the inhabitants lived permanently on rafts or on the man-made islands where the city's vegetables were grown, but every part of Tenochtitlán was accessible by water. The town was laid out in a grid pattern, with a network of canals and bridges dividing the land up into rectangular plots. A companion of Cortés has left this description of the scene:

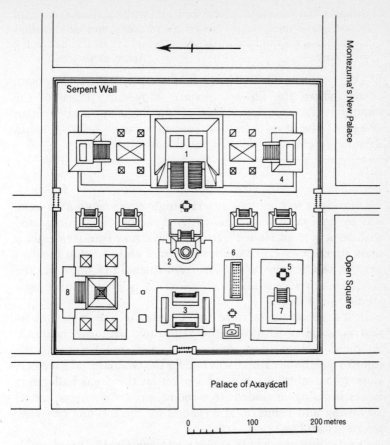

31 Plan of the Great Precinct of Tenochtitlán

1. Shrines of Tlaloc and Huitzilopochtli
2. Temple of Quetzalcoatl   3. Ball court
4. Temple of Tezcatlipoca   5. Platform for gladiatorial combat
6. Skull-rack   7. Temple of the Sun
8. Calmecac

The great city . . . has many broad streets, though among these are two or three pre-eminent. Of the remainder, half of each one is of hard earth like a pavement, and the other half is by water, so that they leave in their canoes or barks, which are of wood hollowed out, although some of them are large enough to hold commodiously five persons. The inhabitants go for a stroll, some in canoes and others along the land, and keep up conversations. Besides these are other principal streets entirely of water, and all travel is by barks and canoes, as I have said, and without these they could neither leave their houses nor return to them, and all the other towns being on the lake in the sweet water are established in the same way. (Anonymous Conqueror)

The city was divided into four sectors, called Cuepopan (Place where the flowers bloom), Moyotlan (Place of the mosquitos), Atzacoalco (Place of the herons), and Teopan (Place of the gods). In the Teopan quarter was the main Temple Precinct, the focal point of the entire city.

The Temple Precinct

The Precinct was laid out as a rectangle covering an area some 380 by 330 yards and enclosed by a masonry wall decorated with serpent heads. The three causeways, now transformed into main streets, converged on this enclosure and ended at fortified gates in the Serpent Wall. The most splendid of these was the Eagle Gate, above which stood a huge stone eagle flanked by a jaguar and a bear.

Inside the precinct were the temples of the most important gods. Here also was the skull-rack with the heads of sacrificed victims lined up in rows, and, not far away, the stone to which the captive was tied for the Gladiatorial Sacrifice. Close to one of the gates stood a court for the ritual ball-game. Lesser buildings included store-rooms, priests' quarters, rooms for fasting and penance, and schools for the training of young priests (31 and 35).

Dominating the whole enclave was the Great Temple with the twin shrines of Tlaloc and Huitzilopochtli sharing a single pyramid. The pyramid measured 100 yards by 80 at its base (not counting the platform which surrounded it) and rose in four or five tiers to a height of about 90 feet. Most of the frontage was occupied by two staircases placed side by side and flanked by balustrades terminating at their lower ends in enormous ser-

32 Stone serpent head, one of a pair which stood at the base of the staircase of the Great Temple in Tenochtitlán

33 Standard-holder of stone
in the form of a seated man.
The pole of the banner passed
between the hands, and the
butt rested in the basal socket.
From Tenochtitlán

pent heads made of carved
and painted stone (32). Towards the upper end of
the staircase the balustrades
changed inclination and became almost vertical, creating
four plinths or platforms. On
each of these was a sculptured
standard-bearer, carved in
the shape of a seated Indian
with his arms folded across his
knees and his hands arranged
to clasp the pole of a banner
made of paper or feathers (33).

The top of the pyramid was levelled to form a terrace on
which stood the temples of the two gods. The main body of each
temple was a box-like structure with no windows and only a
single door, but to give an impression of greater dignity the
buildings were surmounted by high sloping roofs in the shape of
truncated pyramids made of wood faced with stucco. The lower
part of each roof was decorated—the temple of Tlaloc painted
in alternate vertical stripes of blue and white, and the shrine of
Huitzilopochtli ornamented with stone skulls which shone
white against a red background. On top of each roof was a
crest, in the form of shells (for Tlaloc) (34) or butterflies (for
Huitzilopochtli), and on the terrace outside the temples stood
the two stone blocks over which captives were stretched for
sacrifice. Beside these altars burned great braziers, some of them
almost as high as a man.

Close to the main temple was another one, dedicated to
Quetzalcoatl, of which Díaz wrote:

> . . . one of its doors was in the form of a most terrible mouth, such
> as they paint to depict the jaws of hell. This mouth was open and
> contained great fangs to devour souls. By the side of the door were
> groups of devils and forms shaped like the bodies of serpents, and

a little way off was a place of sacrifice, all blood-stained, and black with smoke and dried blood.

Nearby were chopping-blocks and pots filled with water ready for the butchering and cooking of human flesh which formed part of certain rituals.

The inside walls and the woodwork of the shrines were carved with the figures of gods. Blood was splashed everywhere and the smell, Díaz remarked, was worse than that of a slaughter-house in Spain. The idols which stood in these dark and terrifying rooms were carved from wood or stone and were decorated with all kinds of precious objects. Andres de Tapia describes two stone idols, each about three yards high,

> the stone covered over with mother-of-pearl, and over this, fastened with bitumen like a paste, were set in many jewels of gold, and men, snakes, birds and histories [?hieroglyphs] made of small and large turquoises, of emeralds and amethysts, so that all the mother-of-pearl was covered, except in some places where they left it uncovered so as to make work with the stones. These idols had some plump snakes of gold as girdles, and for collars each one had ten or twelve hearts made of gold, and for the face a mask of gold and eyes of mirror [probably obsidian or iron pyrites].

Other images were made of amaranth dough kneaded with human blood and studded with jewels.

34 Stone roof decoration from the Great Temple of Tenochtitlán

Palaces and noble houses

The houses of wealthy Mexicans were multi-roomed structures, often standing on platforms 6 to 40 feet in height, and with walls of stone or adobe covered with lime plaster. Roofs were flat, made of wooden beams covered with planks or shingles, and were frequently spread with earth to form roof gardens. Only the most distinguished men were allowed to build houses with two storeys, and it is doubtful

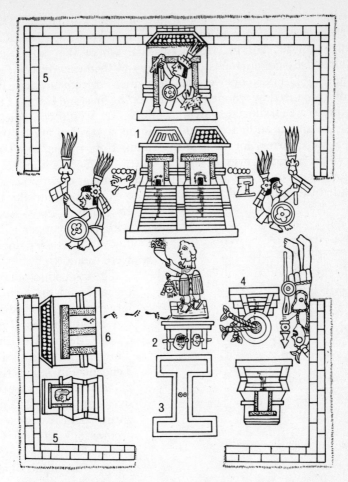

35 Sahagún's plan of the Great Precinct of Tenochtitlán
(Codex Florentino)

1. Main pyramid with shrines of Tlaloc and Huitzilopochtli
2. Skull-rack   3. Ball court
4. Stone for gladiatorial sacrifice
5. Serpent wall   6. Priests' quarters

whether the marshy subsoil of Tenochtitlán could have taken
the weight of anything heavier. All over Mexico, however, the
one- or two-storey building was the rule.

The Aztec house was a self-contained, inward-looking unit.
The walls facing onto the street were blank and featureless, and

all the principal rooms opened onto interior courtyards. This arrangement can be seen in a little group of houses excavated at Chiconauhtla, not far from Texcoco, where the patios are encircled by colonnaded rooms, many of them nearly 200 feet square (36). The floors were of white stucco or cement, and the roofs supported by wooden columns resting on stone blocks. The house of a rich official, Sahagún informs us, would contain an ante-room, an audience chamber, dining and reception rooms, separate quarters for men and women, store-rooms, kitchen, servants' hall, and even a 'place of detention'! Such a house was usually surrounded by a walled garden. Awnings of cotton cloth shaded the patios, and the doorways were closed by curtains or by hanging mats sewn with gold or copper bells. Locks and wooden doors were unknown.

The same kind of lay-out, although on a much larger scale, is found in the royal palaces. Just outside the wall of the Temple Precinct in Tenochtitlán stood the palaces built by successive Aztec rulers. The entire Spanish army was accommodated in the palace of Axayácatl, and many of the soldiers had an opportunity to visit the 'New Palace' which Montezuma built for himself close to the southern wall of the Precinct.

This palace occupied a rectangular site with sides about 220 yards long. It served both as the ruler's private house and as the administra-

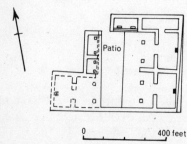

0   400 feet

36 Plan of upper-class dwelling at Chiconauhtla

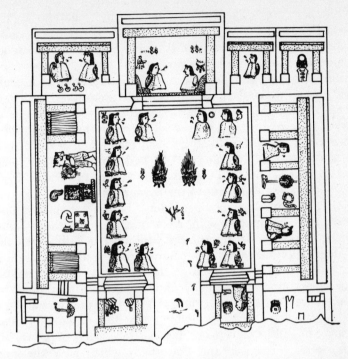

37 The Palace of Nezahualcoyotl at Texcoco (Mapa Quinatzin). The buildings are drawn in elevation without perspective. The king and his son sit in the throne-room (middle top) while chiefs of tributary towns wait in the courtyard. Other buildings include an arsenal (top right) with warriors' costumes hanging up, judges' rooms (top left), store-houses (right-hand side), and a temple or hall for science and music (left, with vertical drum)

tive heart of the empire, and this dual function is reflected in its architecture. The building is said to have had three courtyards, and from a drawing in the Codex Mendoza we know that it was arranged in two terraces or storeys (21). On the upper level, approached by a staircase leading onto a terrace, were the apartments of Montezuma and his household. The ground floor was given over to administration and public works. Here were located the council hall, the appeal court, the treasury and store-houses where tribute was kept, a hall for music and dancing, the quarters for the 3,000 servants and workmen attached to the palace, a jail, an arsenal, and the guest rooms where ambassadors and important visitors were lodged.

The palace was like a small township in itself. The Anonymous Conqueror wrote: 'I walked till I was tired, and never saw the whole of it. It was the custom to place at the entrance of all the houses of the Lords very large halls and sitting rooms around a great patio, and there was one so great that it could hold three thousand persons.' The walls were faced with rare stone or decorated with frescoes, and the woodwork was of carved pine or cedar. There was also an oratory whose walls were covered with gold and silver plaques. The palace at Texcoco was equally grand (37). It had more than 300 rooms, and its upkeep absorbed the tribute labour of 42 villages. Each day 100 turkeys were sent to the royal kitchens.

All these buildings stood in gardens. The palace of Nezahualcoyotl was surrounded by pine trees, interspersed with pavilions, mazes, lakes, and bathing places. Still more beautiful were the gardens of Nezahualcoyotl's country retreat at Tetzcotzinco. An aqueduct carried water from the mountains into a reservoir ornamented with bas-reliefs, and from there it flowed by streams and canals all over the garden, filling the lakes and the bathing pools cut into the living rock. The remains of these basins can still be seen today, but no trace is left of the waterfalls, trees, birdcages, and flowerbeds which gave the king such delight. Montezuma had a similar garden at Huaxtepec which he filled with tropical flowers and young trees sent from the coast.

At both Texcoco and Tenochtitlán there were zoos and aviaries attached to the palace. After describing the birds in Montezuma's aviary, Díaz mentions

38 Carved stone frieze from Tenochtitlán

39 Remains of a coloured fresco showing a procession of warriors, from one of the Malinalco temples

another large house where they kept many idols whom they said were their fierce gods, and with them every kind of beast of prey... most of which were bred there. They were fed on deer, fowls, little dogs, and other creatures which they hunt, and also, I have been told, on the bodies of the Indians they sacrificed. . . . They also had many vipers in this accursed house, and poisonous snakes [rattlesnakes] which have something that sounds like a bell on the end of their tails. These, which are the deadliest serpents of all, they kept in jars and great pottery vessels full of feathers, in which they laid their eggs and reared their young.

To our eyes, even the richest Mexican house would have appeared bare and underfurnished. Wickerwork baskets or wooden chests (some of the chests in Montezuma's palace were said to be 70–80 feet long) held clothes and most of the family's belongings. Everybody, rich and poor alike, slept on reed mats, which were sometimes covered with canopies. Similar mats, placed on a wooden or earthen dais, were the most common form of seat. In the manuscripts are occasional drawings of chairs and four-legged stools but important persons are more often shown seated in *icpalli*, a kind of legless chair (made of rushes or wickerwork) in which the base rested directly on

the floor and the back-rest reached as high as the sitter's head
(24). Other items of furniture included low tables, carved and
gilded screens, wall-hangings, rugs, and braziers in which
burned aromatic woods.

Wall-painting and sculpture

The temples and courtyards of Tenochtitlán were filled with
sculpture, and the walls of both temples and secular buildings
were adorned with frescoes and bas-reliefs (38). Little of this art
has survived the Conquest. Wall-paintings of the Aztec period
have suffered badly, and the best remaining examples are from
two sites a long way from the capital. A damaged mural in one
of the temples at Malinalco shows a procession of warriors (39),
while at Tizatlan, not far from Tlaxcala, are two altars whose
sides are decorated with gods and religious symbols executed in
the same Mixtec-derived style as the figures in the painted books.

Sculpture has fared rather better, and several important
carvings have been preserved. The colossal statue of the goddess
Coatlicue (71) was discovered in 1790 on the site of the main
square of Tenochtitlán, and the same excavation brought to
light the Calendar Stone which, with a weight of 24 tons, is the
largest known Aztec carving. It measures almost 12 feet across,
and the design is a summary of Aztec cosmography (40 and
pp. 153–154). In the centre is the face of Tonatiuh, the Sun,
flanked by claws holding human hearts. At the top of the
outermost band is the date, 13
Reed, when the present Sun was
born, and in the four rectangular panels of the central
zone are the dates on which the
previous Suns were destroyed.
The band around the inner circle
contains the 20 Day-Signs, and
the outer band consists of two
Fire Serpents which meet face
to face at the base of the disc.

The stone of Tizoc (41) is a piece
of commemorative sculpture.
On the upper surface is Tonatiuh

40 The Calendar Stone from
Tenochtitlán

again, and the circumference

41 The Stone of Tizoc

of the drum is carved with reliefs depicting the victories of King Tizoc who is shown, dressed as a god, taking captive the chiefs of the 15 conquered regions whose names are given in hieroglyphs above the scenes of war. This great cylinder is more than eight feet in diameter and was found in the precinct of the main temple. The style of the carved figures is very close to that of the painted figures in Mixtec codices, and it is possible that the work was done by Mixtec craftsmen resident in Tenochtitlán. The link with manuscript painting appears even closer when we remember that Aztec sculpture was often painted in bright colours.

Also from the main temple is a commemorative tablet which was perhaps built into the temple wall. The lower

42 Stone tablet commemorating the work of Tizoc and Ahuítzotl on the Great Temple of Tenochtitlán. The bottom panel bears the date 8 Reed (1487)

part has the glyph 8 Reed (1487), the year in which the new building was finished, and above are two rulers offering a blood-sacrifice from their ear lobes. The two kings are identified by their name-glyphs: on the left is Tizoc, who began the work, and on the right Ahuítzotl in whose reign it was finished. Above the central device is the date 7 Reed (1447) on which Montezuma I made the first efforts towards extension (42).

Many other carvings have been preserved: statues of the gods (43) and of important people, naturalistic renderings of coyotes (44), birds, grasshoppers, and plants, numerous versions of Quetzalcoatl in the

43 Stone figure of Xiuhtecuhtli, the Fire God. 13½ inches high

form of a coiled rattlesnake (70), calendrical inscriptions, Eagle Knights, standard-bearers, models of temple pyramids, and carved vessels for temple use (86 and 87).

All work, from the heaviest to the most delicate, was done without the aid of metal tools. No suitable stone was available in Tenochtitlán, and the most popular material was basalt from the quarries on the lake shore to the south. The blocks of stone for the huge sculptures described above had therefore to be hauled to the city by gangs of men using only ropes, poles, and wooden rollers.

Markets

Every town had its market place, and in the larger cities there were several of them. Even the villages held markets at five-day intervals, and people came in from all the country areas round about, walking up to 10–15 miles each way. The attraction was not just the opportunity to buy and sell, but also the chance to meet friends, to gossip, and to exchange items of local news. The law decreed that nobody might sell his goods on the way to market for fear of offending the market gods, and, although the old gods are no more, the custom has persisted until the present day in parts of rural Mexico.

Certain towns were famous for their specialities: Acolman for edible dogs, Azcapotzalco for birds and slaves, Cholula for featherwork, and Texcoco for its textiles and painted gourds. But the greatest market of all Mexico was in Tlatelolco, close to the main temple, and both Cortés and Bernal Díaz were so impressed by what they saw there that they have left extensive descriptions of it.

Cortés writes: 'There is one square twice as large as that of the city of Salamanca, surrounded by arcades where there are daily assembled more than 60,000 souls, engaged in buying and selling.' The market was under the direct control of the ruler. Pedlars and stall-holders paid a fee to the market superintendent, and inspectors mingled with the crowds, checking the quality of all merchandise and making sure that the prices were not too high. False measures were smashed, and any trader caught passing off shoddy goods had his entire stock confiscated. Thieves, or persons suspected of selling stolen property were taken to the market court where they were tried on the spot by 12 magistrates. Punishment followed directly on sentence, and convicted thieves were beaten to death in the market place where they had committed their crimes. The same court dealt with any disputes between traders.

Each commodity was sold separately. In one part of the square were the vegetable sellers with piles of maize cobs laid out on mats, or with strings of peppers and heaps of fruit, beans, and tomatoes spread out in front of them, each type and quality kept separate from the others. Elsewhere were the sellers of embroidered capes and skirts, agave-fibre sandals, skins of wild beasts, and coarse everyday cloth. From another corner rose the smell of cooked food— roasted meat in various sauces, tortillas and savory tamales, maize cakes, dishes of fish or tripe, and toasted gourd seeds sprinkled with salt or honey. Other

44 Stone sculpture of a coyote

vendors offered ducks, turkeys, or cage birds. In a corner of the square were all the raw materials needed by craftsmen and artisans—bricks and stone, lime, planks and wooden beams for builders, raw cotton for the weaving women, and even (discreetly hidden away in a nearby canal) canoes loaded with the human excrement used by the leather-workers for tanning hides. The housewife could buy cooking pots, reed mats, brooms, bags and baskets, wooden bowls, gourds decorated with lacquer, obsidian mirrors, eye-shadow, herbs for curing sick children, and even love-potions to keep the affections of her husband. Everything imaginable was on sale: paper and paints, glue, feathers, jewels and precious stones, obsidian blades, salt, rubber, bitumen, and resin. . . . The list of items was endless.

Cortés observed that everything was sold by number or by measure, never by weight. The Aztec measures of capacity for such things as maize and other food grains were the *troje* or bin (about 200 tons), and the *tlacopintli* (somewhere between 125 and 140 lb.). The units of length were the hand, the *cemmitl* (the distance a man could span with his arms), and another measurement taken from the ground to the tip of the hand stretched above the head.

Trade was entirely by barter, but certain items came to have generally agreed values and were used almost as we use currency. For expensive things the units of exchange were mantles, copper axe-blades, or quills full of gold dust. Cocoa beans formed the everyday small change, and dishonest people sometimes counterfeited them by making copies in wax or amaranth dough. Prices are not easy to calculate: Sahagún says that a good quality mantle was worth 100 cocoa beans, although only 33 years after the Conquest the price is quoted as 240–300 beans.

Here are some relative values, expressed in terms of mantles (abbreviated as 'm'):

loaf-shaped lump of rubber = $\frac{1}{20}$ m
dugout canoe = 1m
100 sheets of paper = 1m
gold lip-plug = 25m
load of cochineal = 20 or 100m
warrior's costume and shield = about 64m
feather cloak = 100m
string of jade beads = 600m

6

Country Life

There is a natural tendency, shared by Spanish chroniclers and modern archaeologists alike, to concentrate attention on the spectacular aspects of Mexican civilization and to forget that the cultured life of the towns would have been impossible without the taxes and tribute labour of the peasantry. The basis of Aztec economy was agriculture; it was the food surplus produced by the countryside and the provinces which maintained the temples and armies, paid the salaries of the officials, and allowed the nobility to enjoy the comforts of city life.

The most important food plant was maize (which will support a high population at a rather low level of subsistence), and in Aztec times all suitable land was brought into cultivation. Many rural districts were more densely populated than they are today, and the Valley of Mexico supported some 1.5 million people of whom, nearly three-quarters were engaged in agriculture.

The Aztecs, like all the Mexican peoples, had no draught animals, no farm carts, and no ploughs. The land was turned over with a digging-stick, a long-handled tool ending in a broad wooden blade, which served as both spade and hoe (46). With this primitive equipment the Mexicans could not tackle the heaviest soils, and they therefore preferred the rich alluvial silts and the semi-arid soils of the uplands. The Nahuatl language has words for all the different categories of soil from the most fertile, enriched by decayed vegetable matter, to the sterile land made useless by mineral impregnation from the salt lakes.

Farming methods varied from one region to another. In the tropical forests of the Gulf Coast shifting agriculture was the rule. The farmer cleared a patch of forest by cutting down and burning the scrub, after which he cultivated the cleared land for two or three years until the soil was exhausted, and then moved his cornfield to another site, allowing his original plot to revert to forest for at least ten years before being sown again.

In the highlands, fields could be sown for many years in succession with only a moderate period of fallowing. The main danger in upland regions was failure of the rains, causing drought and famine. Starting in 1454, during the reign of the elder Montezuma, there were four consecutive dry years during which the people suffered so badly that many sold themselves as slaves to the Totonacs who paid 400 cobs of maize for a young woman and 500 for a man of working age. The dead were so numerous that they lay unburied for the buzzards to eat. A similar drought struck in the time of Montezuma II, and from the annals we learn that the countryside was also afflicted by plagues of locusts and rats. Sometimes, too, the lake rose and flooded the gardens and low-lying fields. Irrigation was fairly widespread in the Valley and the neighbouring upland regions. Canals and ditches led from the fresh-water streams and the lake to the fields on the valley floor, and one of the farmer's regular tasks was to keep the channels clear. In Montezuma's garden at Huaxtepec, irrigation methods were so well developed that the inhabitants grew tropical plants like vanilla and cocoa under the supervision of 40 gardeners who, with their families, had been brought by the ruler from the Hot Lands where these crops were native. In other regions, especially in the arid lands around the Rio Balsas in western Mexico, it was impossible to raise a harvest at all without irrigation, and the inhabitants were obliged to dig canals or to sow their maize on land which flooded each year.

Chinampas

The most productive plots were the *chinampas*, the gardens made from reclaimed swamps which surrounded Tenochtitlán, Xochimilco, and other lakeside towns. When the Aztecs founded Tenochtitlán on a site which had no agricultural land of its own, they adopted the techniques of land-reclamation already in use among the older Valley tribes. They cut canals through the marshes, and between these canals they heaped up a tangled mass of aquatic plants to create artificial islands surrounded by waterways on at least three sides. On top of this greenstuff was

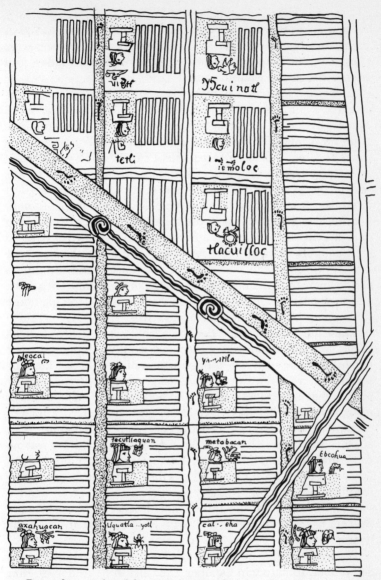

45 Part of an early 16th-century map showing the *chinampa* area of
Tenochtitlán-Tlatelolco. The *chinampa* strips are separated by water,
and the house of the owner stands on a square of solid ground.
Names of owners are given in Aztec hieroglyphs and in Spanish.
Important canals are indicated by wavy lines and curly symbols,
and canal-side streets by rows of footprints

laid fertile mud dredged from the lake bottom, and the sides of the *chinampas* were held in place by posts which served as frameworks for hurdles made of wickerwork. Willow trees were planted on the islands, and their roots helped to consolidate and anchor the newly won ground.

Each *chinampa* was a narrow, rectangular strip of land. The smallest examples measured only 5 by 50 feet, but the usual size was about 300 feet long and 15 to 30 feet wide, and on these more substantial platforms the farmers lived in houses made of canes and reeds. There is a persistent story, which was current as early as 1590, that some of the *chinampas* were floating rafts which could be towed from one part of the lake to another, but it is clear that most of them were of the permanent, non-floating type like the ones in use today. An Aztec map showing part of Tenochtitlán depicts an orderly grid of gardens separated by a network of canals, some of them with footpaths along the banks (45). The plan marks about 400 houses, and the names of the owners are shown in hieroglyphic writing, with later annotations in Spanish. Each property consists of a single house surrounded by six to eight *chinampa* strips.

These gardens provided the city with flowers and fresh vegetables, as well as a portion of the maize supply. All plants except maize spent the early weeks of growth in nursery beds where the seedlings were carefully tended. A layer of mud was spread over part of the *chinampa* and allowed to harden until it could be cut up into rectangular blocks, then the gardener poked a hole in each block, dropped in a seed and covered it with manure. The absence of cattle in the New World meant that there was no stable-manure, and instead the Aztecs used human dung which was collected from the city latrines for sale to the farmers. The seedlings were watered in dry weather and protected against sudden frosts, then at the appropriate time were transplanted to the main beds and mulched with vegetation cut from the swamps.

The sowing times of each crop were regulated (chillis in late September, tomatoes in October, squashes in February) so that the *chinampas* were in production all the year round. If the soil began to show a loss of fertility its goodness was restored by spreading with fresh mud from the lake bed, and with proper maintenance a *chinampa* yielded several crops per year without ever having to lie fallow.

Land tenure and taxation

Every free commoner was a hereditary member of one of the *calpulli*, or clans, which made up the Aztec nation. The clan, not the individual farmer, owned the land, and families were allotted such land as they needed from the common stock. These fields were held in perpetuity and could be passed down from father to son, with the proviso that if the family died out the land reverted to the clan. On the other hand, when a family increased in size and began to need more land this was provided out of the reserve of vacant ground held by the *calpulli*. If, through idleness or decrease in numbers, a family left part of its holding un-worked for two years, a stern warning was issued, and any fields not brought into cultivation during the third year were taken away from the farmer to become clan property again. A clan could not sell or give away its territory—athough it could rent surplus land to another *calpulli*—and any man who went to live outside the clan domain relinquished all claims to his fields.

The free peasant, then, had his rights; but he also had his duties, and one of the most burdensome of these was the need to pay taxes, either in goods or services, to support the whole machinery of the state. Nobles, priests, government officials, and certain warriors were exempt from taxation, and so (at the other end of the scale) were slaves, widows, orphans, and disabled people. The bulk of the direct taxation was paid by the free peasants, who formed about 40 per cent of the total population.

Farmers paid in produce, chiefly foodstuffs and lengths of cloth woven by the women of the household; merchants and craftsmen contributed some of the goods they dealt in or manufactured. This levy went into the ruler's storehouses. Some of it was eventually used to pay governors, ministers, courtiers, royal functionaries, and the army, while the rest was kept in reserve to be distributed at festivals and in times of famine.

In addition the common people were liable for all kinds of services. Each *calpulli* set aside a proportion of its lands to provide revenue for the upkeep of the local temple and schools, and for the welfare services which provided food for travellers and needy folk. The administrative officials of the clan were paid from the same source. These public lands were tilled by peasant farmers, so that local government was supported by local effort.

Other services were for the maintenance of national institutions and the state religion. Menial jobs, like cooking, gardening, and carrying water, were done by tribute labourers. Every year, for example, the families of two entire neighbourhoods were given the task of collecting firewood for the temple of Huitzilopochtli. To pay its share of the costs each family had to donate one large mantle, four small ones, a basket of shelled maize, and 100 cobs. The following year, two other neighbourhoods took over the job.

The people could be called on at will for building or other public works, and in an emergency the whole labour force turned out and was fed at public expense until the crisis had passed.

Hard though life often was, a free peasant could take pride in being a full member of the community with all the rights and obligations which citizenship implies, and could console himself with the thought that some people were much worse off. The most wretched conditions were to be found among the *mayeques*, free men who were not members of any clan and who therefore had no right to a share of the common land. Having no fields of their own, they became share-croppers, renting ground on the estates of the nobility or the temples, and paying their landlords with both services and a share of the crop.

The landowner appointed tribute-collectors, each of whom had charge of some 20 to 50 households, and at harvest time the agents made their rounds, taking away the bulk of the year's crop and leaving the tenant with the bare minimum for his own needs. Because he had nothing left to tax, the *mayeque* was not expected to contribute to state funds or to those of the clan.

Landlords had certain legal rights over their tenants. *Mayeques* were not allowed to leave the estates, and they were often handed over with the land if the estate changed owners. They were also subject to the landlords in civil and criminal matters, but as free men they could not be removed, sold, or treated as slaves who could be put to any kind of work at the pleasure of their masters.

Besides clan property and temple endowments, or 'lands of the gods', there was a third form of public ownership by which fields were assigned to an office rather than to a person. The revenue from these lands paid the salary of the official, and when he died or resigned the ground passed to his successor to be used for the same purpose.

There were, however, private landlords who held property in their own right and not by virtue of office. Senior warriors and noblemen were often given estates, complete with *mayeques* to work them, in conquered territory where their presence made pacification easier by planting Aztec colonies in potentially hostile regions. The greatest landlords of all were the local rulers. Montezuma himself had property in six towns outside Tenochtitlán, and his wife also owned land in various cities. The revenue from privately owned fields went to the landlord rather than the community as a whole, and such estates were passed down from father to son or other male relative. The land could be sold, but only to another nobleman, and if the direct line of descent came to an end ownership reverted to the ruler.

46 Farmer using a digging-stick (Codex Florentino)

Maize

The staple food of all Middle American peoples was maize. It is a plant which gives a good yield, provides adequate nutrition, and can be grown on sandy or rocky ground as well as on the best soil. It can stand a certain amount of desiccation, but a sudden frost in the growing season can destroy the crop overnight, and if such a catastrophe came late in the year, allowing no time for an emergency crop to be planted, the Aztecs faced disaster.

The Mexicans had several varieties of maize, each with its own germination period and keeping properties. Planting took place from March to early May, late enough to avoid the winter frosts but in time to catch the rains which normally began in May and reached a climax in July and August. The best seed corn from the previous year's harvest was put aside in the autumn, then at sowing time it was taken to the temple to be blessed at the feast of the maize goddess, Chicomecoatl, which fell in the fourth month of the Aztec year (13 April–2 May). The seed was then shelled and soaked in water for two or three days to allow it to swell before planting.

In the meantime the farmer prepared the cornfield, breaking up the ground with his digging-stick, and hilling up the earth into little hummocks arranged in rows about a yard apart. A small hole was made in the top of each hill, and at planting time the farmer worked along his rows, carrying the seed corn in a cloth slung over his shoulder and dropping a few grains into each hole which he then closed by pressing down the earth with a sweep of his foot (47). If necessary the seeds were watered, and the soil was turned over two or three times during the growing season.

By mid-July each plant had two or three young ears. All but one of the cobs were removed, and the young tender corn was made into maize cakes which were eaten during the festival of Xilonen, the goddess of young corn and first fruits. By August the cobs had become soft and white, and were ready to ripen. The stalks were bent over just below the ears, and in this position the cobs were left to harden. August and September were critical months, for too much rain during the ripening period could spoil the crop. In the eleventh calendar month (Ochpaniztli, the Month of Brooms) the ceremonies included the sacrifice of a woman impersonating the Goddess of Ripe Corn, and the people performed various other rituals designed to keep the rain away at harvest time. The cobs were yellow and ready for gathering in September, and the farmer returned to his fields to pluck the ears and to tie them up in bundles. Some of the shelled maize was kept in jars around the house, and the rest was stored in great bins made of planks or of wickerwork plastered with mortar (48).

A present-day Maya family of five people eats about 6.55 lb. of maize each day, giving an average daily consumption of some 1.31 lb. per head, and in early Colonial times a tribute labourer was issued with about

47 Planting maize
(Codex Florentino)

48 Filling the storage bins
(Codex Florentino)

2 lb. per day, or twice that amount if he were a farm-worker. Women and children will eat less than men, and an Aztec family would probably have needed a little over 25 cwt. of maize for its own use each year. The yield varied according to the quality of the land, but in Spanish times a figure of 16 bushels per acre was regarded as normal for tributary lands. A family of two adults and three children would therefore need about 3 acres of land to provide maize for its own consumption, and to this we must add the plots set aside for other crops and also extra fields for the maize and other produce taken by the tax collectors.

In the Maya territory today, the average family holding ranges from 10 to 12 acres and requires some 190 days' work a year (including time spent on clearing the forest which was unnecessary in the Valley of Mexico). This labour produces about twice as much maize as the family needs for its own use, and it has been estimated that a family could survive on the fruits of only 48 days' work. Figures for the Mexican highlands were probably not very different, and one suddenly begins to see how Aztec society could allow so many people to withdraw from food-production to serve as priests, warriors, administrators, and craftsmen. Aztec life, with its round of festivals and ceremonial activities, often lasting for days on end, would have been impossible in a land where the agriculture was more demanding of time.

Other crops

Two other plants grew in the corn fields; squashes (belonging to the gourd and pumpkin family) provided shade and conserved moisture around the roots of the growing maize, while beans of many different kinds helped to fix nitrogen in the soil and also supplied the protein lacking in a diet based on maize with little meat and no dairy products.

The other important seed grains, which figure alongside maize and beans in the tribute lists, were chia and huauhtli. Chia (*Salvia hispanica*) is a plant of the sage family whose seeds were used to make a gruel or porridge. They also yielded an oil rather like linseed which was employed in the manufacture of paints and lacquers. Huauhtli (*Amaranthus paniculatus*) produces abundant quantities of a tiny grain which was parched and ground, then used to make gruel or a doughy paste from which the housewife made images to be eaten during the harvest festival. Amaranth was important to the farmer because it ripened at the end of the rainy season and before the maize was ready for harvesting. A good crop of amaranth was therefore some assurance against failure of the maize harvest.

One of the most useful all-purpose plants was the maguey cactus (49) which grows without irrigation on dry and infertile soils, even on those impregnated with lime and salt which were unsuitable for other crops. Maguey will stand great variation of moisture and temperature, is unaffected by the frosts and droughts so dangerous to maize, and is therefore a dependable crop. It grows wild, but was also cultivated in plantations in the drier northern parts of the Valley of Mexico. A maguey plantation was a long-term investment, for the cactus is a perennial requiring up to 10 years to mature. Its leaves were dried for fuel and were employed in thatching; the spines were used to mortify the flesh in blood-letting rituals and also provided sewing needles, especially if extracted with a length of fibre still attached. These same fibres were used to make cloth, sandals, cords, nets, bags, and all manner of household articles. The flower stem was severed close to the base, and the juice which oozed out and collected in the heart of the plant was drawn off and stored in skins or calabashes. Some of the juice was converted into maguey syrup which was used in medicines

49 Maguey plants, with the Temple of the Sun at Teotihuacan in
the background

and as a sweetener for food. Most of the yield, however, was
fermented to become an alcoholic drink called *octli*, which under
the name of *pulque* is still a popular beverage in Mexico. At the
height of its yield a single maguey cactus can give up to 15 pints
of sap each day.

In the garden plots the farmers grew peppers, tomatoes, and
many kinds of fruit, some of which (like avocado, papaya, and
granadilla) can be found in the more exotic European restau-
rants, while others, equally succulent, are unknown outside
Mesoamerica. The prickly pear cactus was cultivated for its
fruit (which contains more seeds than pulp), and in the lands
below 6,000 feet pineapples and sweet potatoes were grown.
Vanilla was planted in the Hot Lands of the Gulf Coast, but
the most important of the tropical crops was cocoa which needs
a hot, damp climate and plenty of shade. It was planted in
groves and protected by taller trees which shielded it from the
sun.

Turkeys and ducks were raised, but the only farmyard animal
was the edible dog which was fed on bread, green corn, meat,
and food that had gone bad. The Mexicans also kept a species
of black and stingless bee which produced both honey and
wax. One of the chroniclers has recorded this apologetic little

prayer which the farmer made to his bees when removing the honey:

I, who come to do this unfriendly act, come compelled by necessity, since I am poor and miserable; thus I come only to seek my maintenance, and so let none of you be afraid nor be frightened of me. I am only going to take you so that you can see my sister the goddess Xochiquetzal—she who is called Precious Branch!

Hunting and fishing

When the ordinary countryman ate meat it was usually the flesh of game animals. The largest creatures in the Valley were the peccary and the white-tailed deer, which was stalked by hunters who crept up, camouflaged in skins, and shot their arrows from close range. Other men lured the animals within range by means of decoy whistles. Small creatures like rabbits, hares, and coyotes were either snared or caught in nets, and larger animals were taken in pitfall traps which were disguised with branches and grass. Deer hides and rabbit fur were important by-products which could be sold to town-dwelling craftsmen for use in the manufacture of sandals and luxury garments. Among the lesser animals which went into the pot were armadillos, gophers, iguana lizards, and wild guinea pigs. The peoples of the Hot Lands also hunted ocelots to obtain the skins which were used to make warriors' costumes and cloaks for Aztec noblemen. Little birds were caught by means of a sticky plant which was hung around the places where the flocks came to feed.

The leisured classes had no need to hunt for food, but they amused themselves by going after quails and pigeons with blowpipes which fired small pellets. Among the gifts which Montezuma gave to Cortés were a dozen such blowpipes, ornamented 'with a great variety of birds, animals, trees, flowers, and various other objects', and with their centres and extremities 'inlaid with gold, and curiously carved'. As a piece of royal extravagance, the pellets were made of gold instead of the customary baked clay.

The lakes provided the country people with both fish and waterfowl. Because of the difference in salinity between the northern and southern lakes both salt and freshwater fish were available, although they rarely grew more than nine inches

50 Catching waterfowl in nets (from an early Colonial map)

long. Traps and fish-weirs were constructed, and the manuscripts illustrate many little scenes of canoes holding fishermen
equipped with three-pronged spears and bag-shaped nets made
of grass fibre (18). While the men worked, they prayed for a
good catch: 'My uncles, the painted ones, the ones decorated
with spots. You who have chins, horns, and fins like beautiful
featherwork or turquoise, come here and make haste to come
for I seek you.'

Some species of birds were non-migratory and could be hunted
all the year round, but in the months from October to March
great flocks of ducks and geese arrived to winter in the Valley.
The fowlers brought them down with curved throwing-sticks,
or else came out in canoes at dusk, making a loud noise to
frighten the birds into nets strung on poles over the water (50).

Peasant houses

The dwelling of an ordinary peasant family was a one-room
rectangular hut with an earth floor, a low open doorway, and
no chimney or windows. The walls were made of stone or, more
often, of mud brick on a stone foundation, or else of wattle and
daub, the traditional building material of the countryside. The
more pretentious houses had flat roofs made of wooden shingles
or of straw laid across horizontal poles, but the most common
form of roof, depicted over and over again in the manuscripts

51 Peasant house of wood and thatch (Codex Mendoza)

(51) was a simple gabled construction made of thatch. Close to the main building stood turkey houses, a sweat house for taking steam baths, and a few bee-hives made from hollowed-out sections of tree trunks with the ends stopped up with mud. The house was primarily a place for eating and sleeping rather than for relaxation. Torches made from pine knots provided the only illumination, and the inside of the house was sparsely furnished. Reed mats served as beds and seats; wooden chests held the family's clothes and possessions, while around the room stood the objects of everyday use—brooms, the husband's digging-stick, seed basket, tools, hunting or fishing gear, the wife's loom, her water jar, cooking and storage pots, a vessel containing maize kernels soaking in lime water, and the stone on which she ground the maize. Each household owned one or more images of the gods, made in wood, stone, or baked clay, and in some huts a cage containing a talking parrot or a small songbird hung on the wall.

The focal point of the room, and the most sacred spot in the house, was the hearth with its three stones arranged in a triangle and supporting the *comal*, a clay disc on which the housewife made the pancake-shaped tortillas which were the family's staple food (7). The cooking fire was of twigs, leaves, maize stalks and dried cactus, but since there was no ventilation the house soon filled with smoke. In this single room, stuffy and smoky, the whole family cooked, ate, and slept.

7

Working Life

In the Aztec hierarchy the craftsmen ranked somewhere between the common people and the ruling classes. They lived in their own quarters of the town, had their own gods and festivals, and formed a distinct section of the community. The artisans who worked in gold, feathers, and gems were known collectively as *tolteca*, and tradition has it that they were the descendants of the Toltecs who dispersed throughout the Valley after the sack of Tula and kept alive their crafts in the smaller towns like Colhuacán and Xochimilco. When the Aztecs conquered the Valley the earlier populations were absorbed and their skills transmitted to the newcomers. Tenochtitlán, as the greatest centre of patronage in all the land, attracted workers from every part of the country. A good deal of the turquoise mosaic and relief-carving, for example, seems to have been executed by Mixtec craftsmen, but it is impossible to say whether or not these foreigners lived in the capital. Somewhat lower in public esteem came the stonemasons, tanners, saltmakers, builders, quarry-men, and carpenters, but we know far less about these workaday craftsmen than we do about their brethren who worked in precious materials.

Metalworking

Copper was occasionally used to make small utilitarian objects like needles, fish hooks, drill-bits, chisels, and axes, but stone and wood remained the usual materials for heavy tools and weapons. Iron was unknown, and the most common metals were gold, copper, and silver, which were used primarily in the manufacture of jewellery and trinkets.

These metals do not occur in the Valley of Mexico and had

therefore to be imported as trade or tribute from distant parts of the country, especially from the mountainous western region. At Cerro del Aguilar, in the territory of the Zapotecs, stone wedges have been collected and traces of fire are still visible at ancient mining sites. Probably the miners heated blocks of ore until cracks appeared, then enlarged the fissures by driving in the wedges until lumps of manageable size could be broken off. Silver came from Tlaxco and Tzompanco (Oaxaca).

The region which produced most gold was the province of Zacatula, on the Pacific coast some 10–12 days' journey from Tenochtitlán, where the Indians used gourds and small wooden troughs to pan gold in the river beds. The same method was employed in the Tuxtepec district of Oaxaca. We know from early Spanish sources that gold was also panned on the east coast, where Grijalva describes how the prospector picked out the grains of gold and stored them in his mouth until he was ready to melt them down on the spot, using a pottery vessel on a fire which he blew up by means of tubes made of hollow reeds.

No tin object has yet been found in the Valley of Mexico, but four lip-plugs made of cast tin are known from Teloloapan in the state of Guerrero. This is very near to Taxco where the ore deposits were exploited in pre-Spanish times, and analysis shows that the metal of the lip-plugs must come from a smelted ore, probably cassiterite, which is still to be found in the area. No crucibles, furnaces, or slag have yet been discovered, but tin can be extracted from cassiterite by packing the ore between alternating layers of wood and charcoal and then heating it to about

52 Metalworker casting an axe. He is using a blowpipe to raise the temperature of the fire, and the molten copper runs out of the furnace-tap into a stone mould. A finished blank lies on the ground beside him (Codex Florentino)

53 Gold mask of Xipe Totec, patron of goldsmiths. It was cast by the 'lost wax method' and originally formed the centrepiece of a necklace. The workmanship is Mixtec, and the find spot a tomb at Monte Alban (Oaxaca)

1,000°C in a pit positioned so as to catch the natural draught.

For working metal the Aztec smith used a furnace heated by charcoal, the draught being supplied by a man blowing through a tube into the embers (52). Copper was added to gold to produce an alloy called *tumbaga* which was cheaper than pure gold, but could be treated to give the appearance of the more precious metal. Solder was made by mixing copper with silver. Copper and tin were alloyed to make true bronze, although the Aztecs do not seem to have realized its superiority over pure copper and showed little sign of taking the technological step which led to the development of a Bronze Age in the Old World.

Few gold objects from the Valley of Mexico have survived to reach museums. From the foundations of the Great Temple of Tenochtitlán came a few gold discs and a nose-ornament in the shape of a butterfly, and in an offering-pit below one of the temple floors were found some copper bells which may have been imported from western Mexico. A few axe or adze blades are also known from the central part of the country.

Motolinía, describing Aztec craftsmen, wrote:

> ... they could cast a bird with a movable tongue, head and wings, and cast a monkey or other monsters with movable head, tongue, feet and hands, and in the hand put a toy so that it appeared to dance with it; and even more, they cast a piece, one half gold and one half silver, and cast a fish with all its scales, one scale of silver, one of gold, at which the Spanish goldsmiths would much marvel.

A few objects with movable parts have been preserved. One is a lip-plug in the form of a serpent with a movable tongue (54), another is a little skull-pendant with an articulated lower jaw from which hang tassels and bells. This pendant was found in the Mixtec country of Oaxaca, and from the same part of Mexico came three bimetallic objects—a pair of small sun discs (half-gold, half-silver) in which the two metals were joined by hammering, and a pendant in the form of a deity wearing an eagle mask over his mouth. In this latter piece, the gold part was made first, then the silver part cast directly on to it without the use of solder.

Precious metals were combined with feathers, or were inlaid with jade or turquoise to produce all kinds of jewellery from necklaces, pendants, and hair-ornaments to plugs for the ears and lips,

54 Gold lip-plug in the shape of a serpent with a movable tongue. Mixtec workmanship, from Tlacolula. Weight 51 grams

and rings for nose and fingers. Vessels were made from gold, silver, and tin; figurines were made by casting; sheet metal was produced by cold-hammering and annealing, and was then cut into shape and decorated by embossing from the back. Some of this sheet metal was used to make small trinkets, but it could be laid over a wooden core to produce large objects like the discs of silver and gold which Cortés sent back to the Emperor

Charles V and which were
described as being the size of cart
wheels or millstones. A more
delicate example of the same
technique is the ceremonial
spear-thrower, now in the
British Museum (94 and 95).

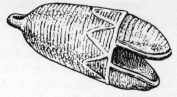

55 Copper bell

The most complicated and
delicate pieces were made by the
cire-perdue, or 'lost-wax', method. For hollow objects, such as
figurines or pendants with movable parts, the goldsmith first
made a core of powdered charcoal mixed with potter's clay.
The core was dried until it became hard, and was then carved
into the desired shape with a small metal blade. The goldsmith
next took purified beeswax mixed with a kind of resin (which
served as a hardening agent), rolled it out to an even thickness and
laid it over the core. Any necessary carving of the wax was done
at this stage, before the outer mould was put on. The wax was
covered thickly with a paste of finely powdered charcoal and
water, then this in its turn was covered over by a layer of coarse
charcoal mixed with clay. Wooden pegs or thorns held the core
in position so that it did not move during casting, and vents
were left in the outer mould to allow the wax to flow out and
the molten metal to come in and replace it. After drying for two
days, the whole thing was heated in a brazier so that the wax
melted and flowed out through the holes to leave a space between
the core and the outer casing. Gold was melted in a crucible,
and then poured into the mould where it filled the space left
by the melted wax and, when hard, gave an exact copy in metal
of the wax original. The mould had to be broken to remove the
contents. Usually the wax model was made freehand, but
certain components (such as wings of birds) were often mass-
produced in open moulds.

Many Mexican objects seem at first glance to have been
made by the filigree process in which metal wire is rolled,
twisted, and soldered to make hollow objects such as beads, or to
produce appliqué decoration on flat surfaces. Closer examination
shows that nearly all these pieces are in the 'false-filigree'
technique, and were in fact made by lost-wax casting (55). Thin
wax threads, which give the appearance of wire, were obtained
by squeezing melted wax through a fine nozzle into cold water.

This thread was used in the same way as true wire, but the wax model was then put into a mould and cast in one operation.

The final job was to polish the surface of the rough casting. If an object made of *tumbaga* is cast in a porous mould the air reacts with the metal to form a layer of dark copper oxide on the surface of the article. This film was removed by immersing the cast in a bath of alum solution, reheating it in a fire, and placing it for a second time in the acid bath. Then it was treated with 'gold medicine' (a mixture of earth and salt) to remove some of the silver present as an impurity in the gold, and to make the surface more yellow before the piece received its final burnishing.

Featherwork

One of the most important guilds in ancient Mexico was that of the feather-workers who lived in the Amantlan quarter of Tenochtitlán where they formed a self-contained community, mixing only with the traders who occupied the neighbouring ward of the city. This association worked to the advantage of both groups, for the craftsmen needed a steady supply of feathers and the merchants had a guaranteed sale for the plumage they brought back from the tropical parts of the country, especially the brilliant green feathers of the quetzal which cannot be obtained in the Valley of Mexico. Great quantities of feathers came to Tenochtitlán as tribute from the hot provinces, and even the birds in the royal aviary were plucked at the appropriate season to provide plumage for the craftsmen attached to the ruler's household.

These men worked privately for the court, making costumes, dance dresses, garments for feast days, and articles to be given as marks of esteem to chiefs and important officials. Other craftsmen worked for the general market, decorating shields, making feather head-dresses and standards, tunics and capes, and all kinds of small things from fans to armbands and tassels.

Rigid objects such as shields were ornamented with mosaic designs made of small pieces of plumage glued to a backing, but in the manufacture of cloaks (which must be supple) or crests and banners (where the feathers must be free to wave in the air) the quills were knotted or sewn into place.

Making a feather mosaic was a complicated process. First the scribe painted the design, full size, on a sheet of paper, then the

56 Feather head-dress given by Montezuma to Cortés

craftsman made a stencil or template from the pattern. A strip of maguey leaf was covered with glue, and onto it was stuck a piece of fine cotton cloth which was left to dry in the sun. Then a coating of glue was applied to the upper surface of the cloth and allowed to harden. The surface of the cotton was now glossy, and the glue-hardened cloth was rather stiff so that it crackled with its dryness. At this stage it was peeled from its maguey backing and laid, like a sheet of tracing cloth, over the paper pattern. The design was then transferred to the stiffened cloth which was further reinforced with a backing of coarse paper before being cut out to form the stencil.

This stencil was used to transfer the design onto a sheet of cotton backed with maguey, and the worker was now ready to apply the first layer of feathers. Since these would be invisible in the finished article he used the cheaper kinds of plumage, some of it dyed to the requisite colour. The feathers were trimmed with a copper knife on a cutting board, dipped into glue, and applied, one by one, with a bone spatula to the cloth, first the outlines in black, then the main parts of the design. Next the decoration was checked against the original pattern, and the cloth, with its layer of inferior feathers, was attached to

57 Obsidian vessel in the form of a monkey. From Texcoco

a board. The final layer was applied in the same way as the first, but this time the workman used precious feathers— green quetzal plumes, eagle down, and the brightly coloured plumage of the cotinga (blue), roseate spoonbill (red), parrot (yellow), and humming-bird (turquoise). A fine ceremonial shield, now in a Vienna museum, is decorated with a blue animal, probably the fabulous creature which was the name-glyph of King Ahuítzotl, on a rose-coloured background. The eyes, claws, teeth, fur, and outline of the animal are made of thin strips of gold (92).

All members of the family helped with the work. The men prepared the stencils and did the cutting and mounting, while the children who were learning the trade prepared the glue from bat excrement or pulverised roots, and the women dyed and sorted the feathers.

No glue was used in the manufacture of mantles and head-dresses. Instead the quills were individually knotted or sewn on to a backing, consisting either of a wooden framework or, in the case of cloaks and tunics, a flexible woven material. A tiara given by Montezuma to Cortés was made of long quetzal plumes woven and sewn on to a backing, trimmed with gold ornaments and with blue, brown, crimson, and white feathers (56). Animal shapes were also produced. The larger ones were carved in lightweight wood, but smaller creatures, such as lizards and butterflies, had skeletons made of maize stalks or strips of paper over which the flesh was modelled in a sort of dough consisting of pulverized maize straw mixed with glue. The surfaces were smoothed with a polisher made of volcanic stone, and then covered over with cotton cloth on which was painted the design to be worked in feathers.

Lapidary work

The favourite gemstones were jade, turquoise, and rock-crystal, but Mexican lapidaries also worked in obsidian, amethyst, amber, bloodstone, carnelian, and a wide variety of coloured materials. Many of these had to be imported: shells were traded from the coasts, emeralds came from Colombia, turquoise and jade from western Mexico.

Hard stones were cut with a copper tool used in combination with water and a special kind of abrasive sand. In working bloodstone, which is so hard that the sand has no effect upon it, the craftsmen first broke up the rock with a stone pounder, then ground the fragments to shape with an abrasive made of water mixed with a powdered stone (emery or flint) of the same hardness as the bloodstone itself. Drilling was carried out with little tubes made of copper, bone, or wood. The final process was the polishing of the surfaces, first with sand, then with a piece of cane.

The lapidaries manufactured a few large objects (such as the animal-shaped vessels made of alabaster and obsidian (57), or the human skulls carved in obsidian and rock-crystal), but more common products were small objects for personal wear or for the use of the gods whose images were dressed with masks and jewellery on festival days.

All sorts of objects were covered with a mosaic of turquoise fragments, often combined with coloured stones and red or white shell. Some of the finest examples have been found in the Mixtec territory where nearly all these materials occur naturally, and it is likely that Mixtec craftsmen introduced the art into the Valley of Mexico.

58 Small shell head of
Xipe Totec

Mosaic ornament was applied to masks, shields and breast-plates, helmets and crowns, sceptres, bracelets, ear-spools, staffs, wooden and pottery vessels, and even to a human thigh-bone which had been notched to convert it into a musical rasp. Mosaic panels were used in composite objects alongside gold and quetzal feathers, and it is recorded that a king of Texcoco had models made in gold and mosaic of every creature which could not be obtained alive for his private zoo.

Cortés acquired several such articles as gifts from Montezuma, and more than 20 of them are still preserved in European museums. Usually the backing is of wood, and the mosaic is

59 Wooden shield, diameter 12½ inches, with a panel of decoration in turquoise mosaic. It was found in the state of Puebla, but the design includes the hieroglyph for the town of Colhuacan. The holes round the edge were for the attachment of a feather fringe

held in place by a cement with a texture like brown gritty sand, although Sahagún records that bitumen or wax were sometimes used instead. The surviving objects include a crested helmet, masks with eyes and teeth of inlaid shell, animal heads, a sacrificial knife with a blade of honey-coloured chalcedony and a handle in the form of an Eagle Knight (85), a breast-ornament shaped like a double-headed serpent (8), and wooden shields decorated with mosaic panels. The finest shield of this

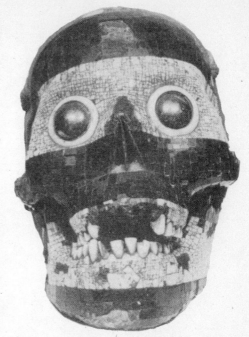

60 Human skull encrusted with a mosaic of turquoise and lignite

type was found in Puebla and has a central panel depicting a mythological scene made up of some 14,000 fragments of stone (59).

Among the more macabre objects are the skull masks. One example, now in the British Museum, is covered with alternate horizontal bands of turquoise and lignite and has eyes of pyrite surrounded by rings of shell. The basis of the mask is a human skull with the back cut away and the inside lined with leather which was originally painted red (60).

Pottery

The potter's wheel was unknown and the craftsmen were ignorant of glazes. All pottery was hand-made, but although the coarse domestic wares could have been produced by non-specialists (perhaps, in country districts, by the farmers during the slack season of the year) the finest vessels, with their varied shapes, thin walls, and tasteful decoration, could only have

61 Aztec Pottery

been made by experts who had undergone a proper apprentice-
ship.

Every Aztec family, however poor, owned some pottery. The
housewife needed a large jar for storing water, a pot for cooking
beans, and another one in which maize could be left to soak
overnight. Tortillas were baked over the fire on a *comal*, a round,
flat griddle with the upper surface smooth and the underside
deliberately roughened to make the distribution of heat more

even. Another specialized shape was the *cajete*, a bowl, usually on three little feet, with the inside roughened by criss-cross incisions (61). It was used for grating chilli peppers. Besides these basic utensils the potters manufactured a whole range of plates, serving dishes, goblets for maguey wine, and special-purpose vessels like cocoa jugs, sauce dishes, and ladles, although only the rich would own a complete dinner service of this kind. All kinds of incense-burners and ritual vessels were manufactured for temple service, and braziers made of pottery were required for both private houses and public buildings (62).

The kitchenware of the ordinary people was rough and plain, but Aztec potters also made a fine ware whose orange or yellow surfaces were covered with cursive patterns in grey or greyish-black lines. The favourite place for decoration was the inside of open bowls, and from about 1350 to the time of the Conquest a gradual change in taste can be recognized. At first the central pattern was usually abstract (though one or two examples have stylized eagles), but on the vessels which were in use when the Spaniards arrived these abstract designs had given place to naturalistic drawings of birds, insects, butterflies, and fish surrounded by ornamental borders (63). During this later period a second class of pottery was introduced and is characterized by black scroll patterns on a glossy red background.

For a person of taste and affluence, however, not even the Aztec best was good enough. The most famous centre of pottery-making in Mexico was the city of Cholula, on the plains of Puebla to

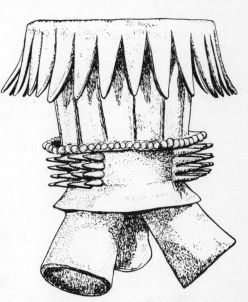

62 Pottery brazier, 42 inches high, found during excavations on the platform of the main temple of Tlatelolco

63 Painted decoration on the inside of a tripod bowl

the south-east of Tenochtitlán, where the inhabitants were of non-Aztec stock and had an artistic tradition of their own. Many Cholulan shapes do not figure in the Aztec repertoire, but what distinguishes Cholula pottery above all is the polychrome decoration in red, brown, black, yellow, orange, blue-grey, and white, which contrasts with the restrained two-colour ornament on Aztec vessels (89). The complex designs of the Cholulan potters include stylized feathers, skulls, flint knives (which suggest some kind of religious symbolism) as well as abstract patterns and figures of gods, men, or animals executed in a style close to that of the painted manuscripts. This pottery was widely traded in Mexico and was popular with the wealthy connoisseurs of Tenochtitlán who preferred it to their own native wares. The fashion may even have started in the Royal household, for it is recorded that Montezuma would eat only from Cholula dishes.

Moulds were not employed in the manufacture of pottery vessels, but the technique was used to produce great quantities of figurines in the shape of temple pyramids (64), gods, human beings, and dolls with jointed limbs. These are dull and unpainted, mass-produced for the popular market, and sold at a price which humble people could afford. Some figurines may

64 Miniature pottery models of temples. The shrines have ornamental roofs and stand on high pyramid-shaped platforms

have been household gods or religious charms, the equivalent of the cheap replicas of saints which can be bought today, while others may have been purely secular and in the same class as the knicknacks and souvenirs which clutter our own mantelpieces (65).

More lively are the designs on the terracotta stamps used to print patterns on something (perhaps cloth or the human body) which has not been preserved in the archaeological record. There are geometric and abstract motives, monkeys and eagles, stylized versions of Quetzalcoatl, the Plumed Serpent, and of other strange figures who may be gods or heroes (66).

Spinning, dyeing, and weaving

All these processes were carried out by the womenfolk. The yarn was spun by hand with the aid of a stick 10–12 inches long (the *spindle*) whose lower end passed through a hole in the centre of a disc made of baked clay (67).

65 Small pottery figurine made in a mould

This disc (or *spindle whorl*) acted as a flywheel, giving extra momentum to the shaft of the spindle as it rotated. Sometimes the lower end of the spindle rested in a little pottery cup which allowed the shaft to turn more freely (68). The woman took the raw cotton in her left hand, and with her right drew out enough to roll into a rough yarn between her thumb and forefinger. The free end of this yarn was attached to the top of the spindle, and when the woman gave the shaft a quick spin the motion was transferred to the thread which was twisted tightly

66 Stamp made of baked clay.
The design shows a monkey

and evenly. When a good length of fibre had been spun, the loose yarn was wound on to the spindle and the whole process repeated.

The finest cloth was made from cotton, all of which had to be imported into the Valley from the plantations in the warmer parts of the country. Cotton fibres are hollow growths attached to individual seeds within the fruit, or *boll*. When the bolls ripen and burst open they are ready for gathering, but the fibres (the *lint*) have to be picked from the seeds by hand. This was a tedious job, and a skilled worker could process only about a pound of cotton in a day. Seeding was followed by *carding* in which the short and useless fibres were combed out. Only the longer ones (usually about one and a half inches) were suitable for spinning.

Second in importance was yarn made from the fibres of the maguey cactus which was cultivated in the Aztec homeland. The leaves were roasted, scraped, squeezed to press out the moisture, and finally treated with maize dough. The resultant thread was coarse and linen-like. Palm-leaf fibre was also employed, and feathers were occasionally twisted on a spindle to make brilliantly coloured yarns. Mexico has no wool-producing animals, but the women sometimes made textiles from yarn spun out of rabbit hair.

In the making of coloured and patterned cloths the yarn was normally dyed before weaving began. A range of colours from celestial to deep blue was produced by dipping the cloth into a bath of indigo, made by the prolonged immersion and fermentation of the leaves of certain shrubs. Weavers and feather-workers used a yellow dye which had to be boiled with alum and salt-petre, both of which

67 Decorated spindle whorls made of pottery

142

are mordants (i.e. substances which themselves do not stain but which help to fix the colour produced by the dye) and it is interesting to note that alum was always sold on the same market stall as pigments and colouring matters. Urine also made a satisfactory mordant.

68 Mother teaching her daughter to spin (Codex Mendoza)

A yellow dye with a green or brownish tinge was extracted from the mora tree. A blue colour was made from acacia leaves mixed with black clay; red came from the seeds of the anatta shrub; green from the matlalquauitl plant; and black from genipa seeds which were collected in the Hot Lands. A further range of colours was produced by successive baths in dyes of different tints. Blue followed by red yielded violet, while blue and yellow gave green.

Of the non-vegetable dyes, red was extracted from the crushed bodies of the cochineal insect which lives on the prickly pear cactus and was deliberately 'farmed' in certain parts of Mexico. About 70,000 insects are needed to make a pound of dye, and it was sold in the markets compressed into bars, either pure or mixed with chalk or flour. It produces a beautiful carmine red, but with a different mordant it will also dye black. Pine soot and red or yellow ochres gave black and a range of earth colours.

Some of the tribes along the Pacific coast extracted purple dye from molluscs related to the species which produced the 'Tyrian Purple' of the Old World. In Oaxaca at the present day the collector prises the Purpura snail from the rocks at low tide and blows into the mouth of the shell. The creature shrinks away from the entrance of the shell which fills up with a frothy secretion. This is dabbed onto the raw cotton, and the snail is replaced, to be 'milked' again after a month or so. The resultant colour is rich and permanent, but a man can dye no more than ¼ lb. of yarn in a single tide.

Several pictures in the codices illustrate women weaving on a simple *belt loom* (69). In weaving, two sets of threads are used— the *warp* (which runs the length of the cloth) and the *weft* (which goes across the fabric, alternately under and over the warp threads). On a Mexican loom, the warp was stretched between two poles, the *warp-beams* (A & B), one of which was attached horizontally to a tree or some other convenient support, while the other was provided with a plaited strap (H) which went around the weaver's back and allowed her to adjust the tension of the warp by altering the pressure of her body against the strap. The method of fixing the warp to the beams is not clearly shown in the codex drawings. Each warp may have been a separate thread, individually tied to the beams, or the Mexicans may have used the Peruvian system in which a continuous warp went backwards and forwards between the poles and was attached to them by cords (C).

In the simplest form of plain weaving, the weft is passed over the first strand of the warp, under the next, over the third, and so on until it has gone the whole width of the cloth. To put it another way, if the warp strands are numbered consecutively across the cloth the weft passes over the odd-numbered threads and under the even-numbered. On the return journey this is reversed; the weft passes *under* the odd numbers and *over* the evens. The same principle is used in darning a sock, and in the most rudimentary looms the weft would have to be laboriously darned over and under each warp thread individually.

Aztec weavers had progressed beyond this stage. If the warp threads can be separated into two sets in such a way that all the odd numbers are raised and all the even numbers are depressed, a clear passage (or *shed*) will be created through which the weft can be passed in one movement (S¹) with a great saving of time and effort. This separation is easy to achieve by means of a roller or *shed-rod* (D) inserted across the warp under every alternate thread. This arrangement will only allow the weft to be passed in a single direction, and if no other device is used the return weft will have to be darned under or over each individual warp.

The difficult part of the problem comes with the creation of the second shed through which the weft makes its return journey. The rod which makes the first shed cannot be pulled out or it would no longer serve its purpose, but somehow the

position of the warp threads
has to be reversed so that the
strands which were formally
depressed are now raised, and
those which were previously
raised are lowered. The
Mexicans solved the problem
by using a *heddle* (E), a second
stick to which alternate warp
strands (i.e. those which went
under the shed-rod) were
attached by long loops of thread
(the *leashes*). While the heddle
lay loosely across the warp between the edge of the cloth and
the roller of the first shed, the
strands to which it was attached
lay slackly in their loops in the
'down' position, and the weft
passed *over* them (S^1). When
the heddle was lifted up above
the warp, it raised the strands to
which it was attached above the
level of the others so that on its
return journey the weft passed
under them (S^2). In this way the
shed-rod and the heddle were
used alternately, the rod forming the first shed and the heddle
the second.

A flat wooden or bone blade
(the *sword* or *batten*) was used to

69 Schematic drawing of a
belt loom, showing the first (S^1)
and second (S^2) shed positions

beat down the weft threads so that they lay close together and
made a good tight weave. Wooden shuttles were also in use
just after the Conquest, but the idea may have been adopted
from the Spaniards.

A loom of the kind described above will produce a two-tone
fabric if the warp and weft are of different colours. With a little
modification, however, it can be made to produce all kinds of
patterns. Further colours can be introduced by breaking off
the weft and joining on another of a different shade. The design

145

can be varied by using several heddles, each of which will give a different pattern, or by altering the arrangement of the leashes attached to a single heddle so that a different set of warp threads is raised.

The chronicles refer to woven capes ornamented with floral and butterfly patterns, or with conch shells, serpent masks, and eagles. Garments were given borders of geometric designs, fancy hems, or fringes, and there were both loose and tight weaves (4). It is clear from the codices that some of these designs were woven on the loom, but tailors and seamstresses also added their quota of decoration, embroidering with a cactus needle those patterns which were too complicated to be woven on the loom. The tailors also made up the fabric into garments. The strip of cloth when it came off the loom was usually not more than two or three yards long and rarely wider than 36 inches, the distance across which the weaver could comfortably pass the weft bobbin from one hand to the other. The tailors were responsible for sleeves, necks and hems, for sewing several pieces of cloth together to make a large garment, and for making individual fittings.

Other industries

Salt Extraction

There was a flourishing salt industry in the northern part of the Valley around the shores of lakes Zumpango, Xaltocan, and Texcoco, whose waters were naturally briny. The highest concentrations of minerals were found not in the water itself but in the surrounding earths which became heavily impregnated, and the best time for salt-working was therefore the dry season when the water level dropped and parts of the lake bed were exposed.

The earth was collected and piled up into hillocks which were then washed to obtain a concentrated salt solution. The brine which resulted from this process was poured into earthenware jars and heated to evaporate the water. The residue was a dry, darkish-coloured salt which was traded all over the country in the form of compressed balls, blocks, and round cakes about the size of a loaf of bread. It was also sold as jars of granulated salt. The Tlaxcalans, however, had to do without salt because their Aztec enemies controlled the supplies and forbade all commerce.

Obsidian Chipping

Obsidian, a black glass produced naturally by volcanic activity, was used for making spear-heads and knives. The workman sat on the ground, gripping between his feet a cylindrical block of obsidian about eight inches long and as thick as a leg or arm. Thin slivers, or *blades*, were detached from the core by means of a crutch-shaped wooden flaking tool. The worker placed the tip close to the edge of the upper surface of the block (which had previously been roughened with an abrasive to stop the tool from slipping) and rested his chest on the cross piece. A downward jerk of his body applied a sudden pressure which forced off a thin parallel-sided flake from the core, and the process was repeated until a stock of blades had been accumulated and the core was so reduced in size as to make further working impossible. A single workman could manufacture about 100 blades in an hour.

Freshly broken obsidian is as sharp as glass, and the blades were ready to be used as knives or as edge-pieces on warriors' sword-clubs without any further retouching. In the manufacture of javelin-heads and similar tools, wider blades were trimmed to shape and then thinned by secondary pressure flaking on the faces.

The travelling merchants

The travelling merchants, or *pochteca*, formed a separate class within Mexican society and are not to be confused with the pedlars and petty traders who sold their wares in the market places of the Valley. The *pochteca* engaged only in foreign trade. They were organized into powerful guilds with their own privileges, and by the time of the Conquest there were corporations of *pochteca* in more than a dozen highland cities.

The merchants lived together in their own quarters of the city (there were seven such districts in Tlatelolco, including one called Pochtlan) and kept very much to themselves. They married within the profession, and only the sons of merchants were allowed to become *pochteca*. They had their own courts which were outside the state system and dealt with both civil and commercial offences among the trading community. Their judges pronounced and executed all sentences including the death penalty for serious crimes. The merchants also had their own god (Yacatecuhtli, the Lord Who Guides), and at the great festival of Huitzilopochtli, which was held in the 15th month, the traders were privileged to sacrifice slaves immediately after the warriors had offered their captives.

In Tenochtitlán the guild was ruled by a small group of three (or perhaps five) experienced merchants who had grown too old to make long and dangerous journeys. They served as advisers and administrators, representing the corporation in its dealings with the ruler, regulating market prices, and presiding over the ceremonies which accompanied the departure and arrival of the caravans.

Since a trading mission represented a vast capital outlay and might spend years away from home, nothing was left to chance. Departure was timed to coincide with a lucky date, if possible the day 1 Serpent which was particularly fortunate for merchants. On the day before setting out, both the *pochteca* and those relatives who were to be left behind washed their heads and cut their hair—a thing they would not do again until the travellers had returned safely. On the eve of departure offerings were made to the gods, and the corporation gave a feast for those about to set off. The senior merchants reminded the travellers of their duties to each other and to the gods, and warned them about the trials of the journey—the rough roads, deserts, swollen rivers, fatigue, unseasoned food, stale tortillas, soggy maize, and foul water. The farewell speeches did not attempt to gloss over the risks: 'We know not whether thy mothers and fathers lose thee forever. Perhaps thou goest for good; perhaps thou goest to be lost . . . Yet know and carry in thy heart that thou goest fortified by the tears and compassion of thy fathers and mothers' (Sahagún).

Meanwhile everything had been prepared for the journey. Porters were engaged, and the merchandise and rations were assembled at the house of the caravan leader. Trading was organized on a corporate basis, and the caravans took goods contributed by non-travelling members of the guilds and even by women traders. The ruler himself was not above making an investment, and Ahuítzotl's stake in one expedition amounted to 1,600 large capes and other rich clothes. In their packs the *pochteca* carried raw materials from the highlands and all sorts of manufactured goods: gold ornaments, lip-plugs of rock crystal and tin, rabbit fur, medicinal herbs, sewing needles, cochineal, alum, razors made of obsidian blades with leather handles, clothing, and pottery.

All these were loaded into canoes which slipped unobtrusively out of the city by night. Farewells were kept short: 'None entered the women's quarters, neither did any turn back or look to one side. If perchance he had gone forgetting something, he might no more come to take it, nor might they still go to offer it to him' (Sahagún). On the march the long line of porters was accompanied by experienced merchants and by apprentice youths making the trip for the first time (26). An armed escort was in attendance to keep off robbers and, where necessary, to force trade upon unwilling partners.

A Mexican trading mission was equipped like a small army, and on occasion behaved like one. If a foreign tribe refused to trade this was regarded as an unfriendly act which could lead to war, and history shows that trade was often the prelude to conquest. The merchants acted as spies, assessing the wealth of the land and looking out for military weakness which could be exploited later. Often the *pochteca* deliberately provoked the local population in the hope of starting a war, and in the time of Ahuítzotl a group of Mexican traders had to withstand a four-year siege in the city of Quauhtenanco on the Pacific coast. When eventually the ruler sent an army to relieve the *pochteca* he learned that the merchants had fought their way out of the town and had conquered the surrounding district by their own efforts.

Aztec merchants sometimes visited the country of the Mixtecs and the Totonacs, but the most important trade route led to the Hot Lands further south. The caravans from the highland cities first made for Tochtepec, an entrepôt town where all the corporations owned store-rooms and rest-houses for their members (3). The wealth of the province of Tochtepec, which contained 22 towns, can be gauged from the list of tribute which it paid to Tenochtitlán. Every 80 days the province contributed 2,800 items of clothing, and once a year it sent the following commodities:

40 lip-plugs of gold and
   semi-precious stone
80 handfuls of quetzal plumes
7 strings of jade
3 large pieces of jade

100 jars of liquidamber resin
200 loads of cocoa beans
2 necklaces of gold beads
4 bunches of quetzal feathers
  bound in gold
24,000 bunches of mixed red,
  green, and blue feathers
16,000 balls of rubber
1 rich warrior's costume
1 feather shield
1 gold shield
1 feather head-dress
1 gold diadem
1 gold head-band

From Tochtepec the merchants visited friendly cities, while certain brave traders, the 'disguised merchants' who spoke foreign languages and could pass for natives, slipped into hostile territory to spy out the land.

East of Tochtepec, trade was the monopoly of the *pochteca* of Tenochtitlán, Tlatelolco, Quauhtitlan, and Uitzilopochco. One major route led to the Pacific coast and the provinces of Ayotlan and Xoconochco. The other route went northwards to Xicalango, a trading port in the territory of the Chontal Maya who controlled the sea trade round the coasts of Yucatan and whose canoes brought jade, tropical plumage, and jaguar skins from the Maya hinterland, as well as coral and sea shells from the coast. Nahuatl was the *lingua franca* of the traders and at the time of the Conquest was still spoken in Xicalango, even though Maya was the native language of the countryside.

Not everyone survived the journey. If a merchant died far from home, his companions bound his body to a carrying-frame and dressed it in ornaments and a paper stole. The face of the corpse was painted (black around the hollow of the eyes, red on the lips) and the body was painted with white stripes. The dead man was carried to a mountain top where the corpse, still on its frame, was propped up and left. When the caravan returned home the family of the dead merchant made an effigy which was cremated as if it had been the actual body.

For their homecoming the traders tried to choose a favourable day such as 1 or 7 House, and entered the city secretly at night, with their goods hidden in a covered boat so that no-one could see their riches. The merchandise was not taken to the house of the trader himself but was left with a friend or relative, and by dawn everything was stowed away out of sight.

Secrecy and evasiveness were characteristic of merchant life. As a class the *pochteca* were wealthy, privileged, and politically important, but nothing of this was allowed to show on the surface. Except on feast days they wore simple capes of maguey fibre, with no insignia to rouse the envy of the warriors and officials, and if one were to meet a merchant on the road he would deny all ownership of his goods, saying that he was transporting them on behalf of another member of the guild.

The *pochteca* had power, but in a society which valued public service above private gain they tried not to draw attention to themselves. As Sahagún's informants put it, 'They were very moderate; they did not exalt themselves. They greatly feared notoriety, the praise with which one is praised.'

8

Religious Life

To the Aztecs the gods were ever-present and all-powerful. It was they who controlled man's fate, who sent or withheld the spring rains at their pleasure, who watched over every day and every hour. They represented all that was good or evil in life; the stability of the universe was in their hands, and on their goodwill depended man's very existence.

Aztec religion was one of propitiation. The individual worshipper was not striving for spiritual perfection or personal salvation, but was trying to influence the natural forces so that they worked in his favour or for the good of the community as a whole. In the words of Alfonso Caso,

> So great was the importance of religion for the Aztec people that we can say without exaggeration that their existence revolved totally around religion. There was not a single act of public or private life which was not coloured by religious sentiment. Religion was the preponderant factor, and intervened as *causa* (motive, origin, reason), in those activities which to us seem most alien to religious feeling, such as sports, games and war. It controlled commerce, politics, conquest. It intervened in every act of the individual, from birth until the moment when the priests cremated his corpse and interred the ashes.

Creation and the universe

According to Aztec mythology the two most ancient gods were Ometecuhtli and Omecíhuatl, Lord and Lady of the Duality, or Lord and Lady of Our Sustenance. The divine pair had four sons to whom they entrusted the creation of all the other gods, and also of the world and the races of man who were to inhabit it.

The sons of the primordial couple were the four Tezcatlipocas: the Red Tezcatlipoca (who became known as Xipe Totec), the Blue Tezcatlipoca (who was identified with Huitzilopochtli, the national god of the Aztecs), the Black Tezcatlipoca (the only one of the quartet to retain his original name in everyday usage), and Quetzalcoatl (who took over the functions and attributes of the White Tezcatlipoca of the west). Of the four gods, the two most important are Quetzalcoatl, a benevolent deity and friend of mankind, and Tezcatlipoca, an omnipotent being who was god of darkness and sorcery. These two divinities were rivals, and during the course of their struggle for supremacy the universe was created and destroyed four times.

One tradition tells the following story:

When the first creation took place, Tezcatlipoca transformed himself into the sun. The earth at this time was inhabited by giants who lived on acorns, berries, and roots. Quetzalcoatl, who could not bear to see his enemy rule over the universe, took his staff and knocked Tezcatlipoca out of the sky, but in a fit of rage the defeated god turned himself into a jaguar and destroyed the earth. This cataclysm took place on the day 4 Jaguar.

Quetzalcoatl then took Tezcatlipoca's place in the heavens and initiated the second age of the world. Creation began anew,

70 Sculpture of Quetzalcoatl. The face of the god peers through the open jaws of a feathered serpent

and the earth was peopled with men who ate only pine nuts. This era came to an end on day 4 Wind when Tezcatlipoca overthrew Quetzalcoatl and sent a great wind which devastated the earth. The few surviving men were changed into monkeys.

Next Tlaloc, the God of Rain, took his turn as sun, but Quetzalcoatl sent down fire which consumed the earth. The day was 4 Rain, and by the end of it all men had perished, apart from a few who were transformed into birds. Finally Chalchihuitlicue, the Water Goddess, took over the sun's responsibilities. She fared no better; on the day 4 Water her universe was destroyed by floods, and such men as were not drowned were changed into fishes.

This story appears in a Nahuatl manuscript written in 1558 but incorporating a much older oral tradition. Its anonymous author maintains that the First Sun was created 2,513 years before the time of writing, but in another version, in which the sequence of events is slightly different, the beginning of the world is placed about 20,000 years ago.

Both versions agree, however, that at the end of each era the sun was destroyed and the earth depopulated. The Fifth Sun (i.e. the present age of mankind) began with a meeting of the gods at Teotihuacán. It was decided that one of their number should sacrifice himself to become the new sun, and a humble god, poor and covered with boils, cast himself into the brazier and was reborn as the sun. But this was not enough; the sun hung in the sky, but it would not move. In desperation all the other gods sacrificed themselves, and at last the sun began to move across the heavens. The fifth age—the era of Tonatiuh, the Sun God—had begun, but like the others its end was fore-ordained. On a year ending with the day 4 Motion, the world would be destroyed by earthquakes.

Having created a sun, it remained to create mankind again. This task was given to Quetzalcoatl who journeyed to the underworld and brought back the bones of previous generations. In escaping from the god of the underworld, Quetzalcoatl slipped and smashed the bones he was carrying, but, making the best of a bad job, he sprinkled the fragments with his own blood and thus transformed them into men. Because the fragments of bone were of different sizes, men and women are not all alike.

The Mexicans imagined the universe as having both a vertical and a horizontal structure. The earth was a large disc entirely surrounded by water, and all beings were assigned to one of the four directions, each of which was associated with one of the four creator gods (82). The centre point was ruled over by Ometecuhtli and Omecíhuatl, the original divine pair, and was the area where the horizontal and vertical universes intersected. To put it another way, the central 'direction' was up and down—up to the 13 heavens (arranged in layers one above the other), and down to the underworld with its nine hells.

The gods

Aztec religion was polytheistic, based on the worship of a great number of gods and goddesses, some of whom (like Tlaloc, Tezcatlipoca and Quetzalcoatl) had long been known in the Valley of Mexico. Others were adopted from conquered peoples, and by the reign of Montezuma II the imported gods had become so numerous that a special temple had to be built for them close to the shrine of Huitzilopochtli in the capital. The priests and philosophers tried to present these foreign deities as aspects of already existing gods and in this way to assimilate them into the national pantheon, but popular belief worked in the opposite direction, treating as gods in their own right what to the priests were simply different manifestations of the same god.

Huitzilopochtli, Left-handed Humming Bird or Humming Bird of the South, was the national god of the Aztecs and, unlike the other Mexican deities, had no great following outside Tenochtitlán and Tlatelolco. He had been the tribal god during the period of wandering, and as the Aztecs had increased in importance so had his cult, until his only rival was Tlaloc, the Rain God, with whom he shared the place of honour on top of the great pyramid. The Aztecs, in particular the warrior classes, considered themselves his chosen people.

His mother, so the legends tell, was Coatlicue, the old Earth Goddess. She had already given birth to the moon and stars when one day, while sweeping the temple, she found a ball of feathers which she carefully tucked into her bosom. When she came to look for the ball afterwards she found that it was gone, and at the same time realized that she was expecting another child. Her sons and daughters found this tale anything but convincing and, ashamed of their mother's dishonour, they resolved to kill Coatlicue and her unborn child. While they were still making preparations Huitzilopochtli was born, and with the help of a fire-serpent(73) he defeated and killed all his brothers and sisters.

From the moment of his birth, therefore, Huitzilopochtli was a warrior god, fit patron for a militaristic nation like the Aztecs. But at the same time he was a manifestation of the sun, and as such his battle against the forces of night was never-ending. Each morning the sun was born anew; each night his combat with the moon and stars was re-enacted. A song in honour of the god begins with the words

Huitzilopochtli,
young war chief—
none have equalled
me.
Not for nothing
have I
taken the
cloak of yellow
feathers.
Through me hath
the sun risen. . . .

71 Statue of the goddess Coatlicue, from Tenochtitlán

But what if the god should grow weak, and fail in his task? The outcome was terrible even to think about, for if one morning the sun did not rise mankind and the universe itself would come to an end.

It was essential that Huitzilopochtli should remain strong and vigorous, that man should give nourishment to the sun to strengthen him in his struggle against darkness. The most precious food which man could provide was life itself, the magical substance found in human hearts and blood, the 'divine liquor' which was offered on the battlefields and altars. And therein lay the justification for human sacrifice.

The more important the deity, the wider were his responsibilities. Quetzalcoatl (Plumed Serpent) has already been mentioned in his role as a creator god, but under the name Ehécatl he was also the Wind God, in which guise he appeared not as a feathered serpent but as a personage wearing a beak-shaped mask over his face (72). His calendar name was Ce Acatl (One Reed), but he was also known as Lord of the House of Dawn (i.e. of the planet Venus, which appears for a while as the evening star and then disappears, to re-emerge as a morning star). In his capacity as Venus god he had two aspects, represented in the morning by Quetzalcoatl and in the evening by Xolotl, the dog-headed monster (75). This duality made him the god of twins, to whom barren women prayed for children, and as the creator and

72. Statue of Ehécatl, the Wind God, found at Calixtlahuaca

benefactor of mankind he was patron of crafts and of all forms of knowledge. The *calmecac* schools were under his protection.

To the priests and theologians he was a single god with a number of different aspects. The uneducated classes, however, considered the separate aspects of Quetzalcoatl as independent gods, each of which had his own title, attributes, and sphere of influence.

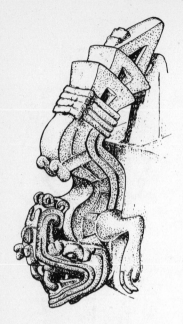

73 Stone carving of a
firesnake

One school of philosophy held that all the gods were just different manifestations of a single supreme being, the giver of life, who had begotten the universe and the gods and men who inhabited it. The original creator couple, Ometecuhtli and Omecíhuatl, were themselves aspects of a single deity, called Ometeotl (God of the Duality) who was at the same time both masculine and feminine. This omnipotent but unknowable divinity was worshipped under the name of Tloque Nahuaque (Lord of Everywhere). Of all the gods he is the only one who is never shown in paintings or sculpture. His cult had no appeal to the masses, although Nezahualcoyotl, that most philosophical of rulers, built a temple in his honour at Texcoco. No idol was placed inside the shrine, for Tloque Nahuaque was an invisible and intangible god whom no man had either known or seen. Another of his titles was Moyocoyani (He Who Gives Existence to Himself); as creator of the world he had no parents, for he had existed ever since time began.

Such philosophical speculation had little effect on popular religion. The peasants remained obstinately attached to their local rustic gods who protected the harvests and the food supplies. Their names were often derived from the regions where they were worshipped—like Tepoztecatl, the god of Tepoztlan, or Yautecatl from the town of Yautepec—and they were so numerous that they were collectively known as the Four Hundred Rabbits. As agricultural gods they came into their own at the time of the harvest festivals when *octli* was drunk freely, and so by extension became the gods of drunkenness. Each town or village had its god, and each class, profession, or trade guild had its own patron.

Among this multitude of gods and godlings a number stood out above the crowd. They were the important divinities, the creator and solar gods on whom the universe depended, and the agricultural gods who controlled the seasons and the crops.

Of the latter, the most powerful was Tlaloc, the Rain God. He is easily distinguished by the spectacle-shaped mask which rings his eyes, or by his mouth-mask which looks like a fringe of curved tusks (74). His dress is usually blue or green (the colours of water) and he is often depicted with stylized raindrops pouring from his hands. The Tlaloque, the innumerable mountain gods who controlled rivers, wells, snow, and hailstorms, were probably local manifestations of Tlaloc himself.

His title means 'He Who Makes Things Grow', and he was the god who sent down rain

74 Small stone sculpture of Tlaloc, the Rain God

for the growing crops. Usually he was well disposed towards mankind, but if he were angered he could retaliate by sending floods, lightning, freezing sleet, or out-of-season rain which caused mildew in the storage bins and made the crops too wet to gather.

In the first and third months of the year, little children were sacrificed to Tlaloc on the mountain tops. Their tears symbolized falling rain, and the more they wept the better were the chances of rain when it was needed. In the sixth month the priests bathed in the lake on four consecutive days, churning up the water and imitating the cries of birds. People who had committed misdemeanours were thrown into the water and pushed back when they tried to escape, and as a climax to the festival many captives were slain and their hearts piled into a canoe which was poled out into the lake and there sunk.

75 Front and rear views of a statue of Xolotl

Another god of fertility was Xipe Totec (Our Lord the Flayed One) whose cult was introduced from the country of the Huastecs. He was one of the creator gods, identified with the Red Tezcatlipoca, and his clothes and ornaments were red. His face, too, was painted red with a decoration of yellow bands, and he is often shown wearing a flayed human skin, symbolizing the covering of new vegetation with which the earth was clothed each springtime (76). This skin dried a golden colour, and Xipe was therefore the patron of goldsmiths as well as the god of spring growth. Some of the prisoners dedicated to him were tied to a high wooden framework and shot to death with arrows so that their blood dripped to the ground like life-giving rain.

Other captives suffered the gladiatorial sacrifice. The victim was tethered to a huge round stone which stood in the main square of the city. He was issued with dummy weapons (four wooden balls, four pinewood cudgels, and a sword-club edged with down instead of obsidian blades) and fought in turn four knights who were armed with real weapons (77). If they failed to kill him, he was dispatched by a fifth, left-handed, warrior. The corpse was flayed and the captor kept the skin for 20 days, either wearing it himself or lending it to others in return for

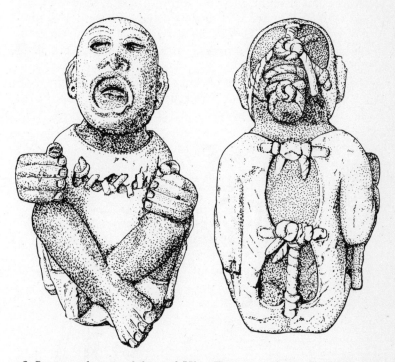

76 Stone sculpture of the god Xipe Totec wearing a flayed human skin. The flesh of the god was painted red. The front view shows the gash in the victim's breast (neatly sewn up again) through which the heart was extracted, and also the way in which the wearer's own face shows through the stretched mouth of the skin mask. The rear view shows how the skin was tied on at the back

gifts. By the end of this period, so Sahagún's informants told him, the people wearing the skins 'stank like dead dogs'.

Another important god was Quetzalcoatl's rival, Tezcatlipoca (Smoking Mirror), an all-powerful deity who both gave and took away life. He was eternally young, invisible 'like the darkness, like the mind', and in his obsidian mirror he could see everything that happened in the world. He was the god of the night sky, and hence the patron of sorcerers and robbers, and was also a war god, the 'warrior of the north' and the protector of the *telpochcalli* schools where the young warriors were trained. His disguise was a jaguar, and his fetish was a knife of flint or obsidian.

In the manuscripts the god is shown with his face painted black as befits a night god and with horizontal stripes on his cheeks to mark him as one of the four sons of the creator couple. As a war god, his hair is cut in the warrior style, and he carries a shield and weapons. His mirror is worn at his temple or in place of one of his feet (78).

The most dramatic piece of Aztec sculpture to come down to us is a statue of Coatlicue (Lady of the Serpent Skirt), the Earth

77 The Gladiatorial Sacrifice. The victim, armed with dummy weapons, is tethered to a large stone and made to fight a succession of warriors armed with real weapons (Codex Magliabecchiano)

Goddess who was the mother of the moon, the stars, and Huitzilopochtli (71). She wears a skirt of intertwined serpents held up by a belt in the form of a snake, and as mother and nurse of the gods she is shown with her breast bare. Her hands and feet have claws, for she feeds on corpses, and on her chest hangs a

78 The god Tezcatlipoca, from a Mixtec manuscript (Codex Borgia)

skull-pendant suspended from a necklace made of alternating human hearts and hands. Her head has been severed, and from the neck flow two streams of blood represented by snakes whose heads meet in profile to form a grotesque caricature of a face. Her other aspects were Cihuacoatl, goddess of child-birth, and Tlazolteotl (Eater of Filth) to whom penitents confessed their sins.

The solar calendar

For ordinary purposes the Aztecs used a 365-day calendar based on the solar year and divided into 18 months of 20 days, with the addition of 5 days, called the 'hollow' days, which were thought to be unlucky. This calendar, like the Sacred Almanac described on pages 165–166, was not an Aztec discovery but was part of the heritage shared by all the civilized nations of Mexico. By the sixth or seventh centuries, Maya astronomers had calculated the length of the sun's year as 365.2420 days (the modern figure is 365.2422), and had invented a correction formula more accurate than the system of leap years used in the Christian calendar. The Aztecs must certainly have known the true length of the year, and there are hints that the adjustment was made by adding a sixth 'hollow day' every four years.

Mexican astronomers had also observed the moon and the constellations, to which they gave names just as we give names to the signs of the Zodiac. The Great Bear was known as the

79 Priest making astronomical sightings through a pair of crossed sticks on a temple platform

Tiger; the Little Bear was called after an S-shaped loaf of bread, and, by a curious coincidence, the constellation which we call Scorpio was also called Scorpion in Mexico. The priests had also measured the 584-day Venus year based on the apparent revolution of the planet, and were able to forecast eclipses. The data had been collected over the centuries by astronomer-priests using only the simplest apparatus. They set up a pair of crossed sticks inside a temple whose situation on top of a pyramid allowed a clear view of the horizon, and, sighting from this fixed point, noted the places where the various heavenly bodies rose and fell in relation to some natural feature like a mountain peak or prominent landmark (79). To calculate the synodical revolution (or 'year') of a particular planet the observer had only to count the days until it reappeared in its original position on the horizon.

The year was named after the Sacred Almanac day on which it began, and the names of the 18 months show how the solar calendar was the basis of both the agricultural and the ritual year:

1 Stopping of the Water	10 Fall of the Fruits
2 Flaying of Men	11 Month of Sweeping
3 Lesser Vigil	12 Return of the Gods
4 Greater Vigil	13 Feast of the Mountains
5 Drought	14 Quecholli (a species of bird)
6 Eating of Bean Porridge	15 Raising of the Feather Banners
7 Lesser Feast of the Lords	16 Fall of the Waters
8 Great Feast of the Lords	17 Severe Weather
9 Offering of Flowers	18 Growth

The more fanciful names are taken from the monthly ceremonies and festivals, but the others demonstrate the farmer's preoccupation with seasons, growth, and, above all, with rainfall— a reminder that even in highland Mexico drought and famine were ever-present risks. Sahagún reports that in the sixteenth century the Aztec year began on 2 February by our calendar.

The 'hollow days' were a time of ill omen. 'These five days [wrote Sahagún] they held as of evil fortune and unlucky. They said that all who were born in them had evil outcomes in all their affairs and were poor and wretched. . . . They dared do nothing in these days. Especially did they abstain from quarrelling, because they said that those who quarrelled in those days always remained with that custom.' During these unfortunate days no festivals were held and no important business was done for fear it would turn out badly.

Astrology and the Sacred Almanac

The Sacred Almanac which the priests used in divination was called the 'Count of the Days', and was a 260-day cycle based on a combination of the numbers 1–13 with the 20 named days of the Mexican calendar. Each day had its own sign or hieroglyph:

cipactli: alligator	*ozomatli:* monkey
xochitl: flower	*itzcuintli:* dog
quiautl: rain	*atl:* water
tecpatl: flint knife	*tochtli:* rabbit
ollin: motion, or earthquake	*mazatl:* deer
cozcaquauhtli: vulture	*miquiztli:* death
quauhtli: eagle	*coatl:* serpent
ocelotl: ocelot	*cuetzpalin:* lizard
acatl: reed	*calli:* house
malinalli: grass	*ehecatl:* wind

There are 260 possible pairings of name and number, and the Sacred Almanac can be imagined as two intermeshing cog wheels, one with 13 teeth (the numbers), the other with 20, representing the days (80). If the first day of the cycle is One Alligator, the second will be Two Wind, the third Three House, and so on until the wheels have returned to their original positions. The entire process will take 260 days (13 × 20), after which the next Almanac Year will begin with One Alligator again.

The 260 days of the Almanac Year were divided into 20 groups of 13, each of these 'weeks' beginning with the figure 1 in combination with a different day sign. Returning to our

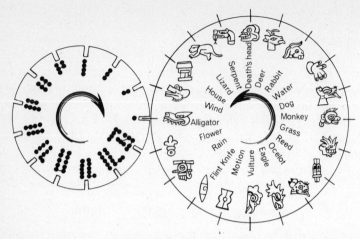

80 Diagrammatic representation of the 260-day Almanac Year. The
20 named days intermesh with the numbers 1–13

cogwheel diagram, we can see how the system worked. The first
'week' began with One Alligator and lasted for 13 days, by
which time the number wheel had made one complete revolution and the day wheel moved on 12 more places to bring the
reed sign opposite the number 1. Thirteen days later the
death's head sign would be paired with number 1, until by the end
of an Almanac Year each of the day signs had taken its turn in
the initial position.

The Almanac calendar was quite independent of the Solar
Year and was used only for astrology and divination. The
information was codified in the pictorial diagrams of the
tonalamatl (Book of the Days), and in making their predictions
the priests had to study and weigh up the different (and often
contradictory) elements which could exert an influence on any
particular day (81).

Each of the day-signs had its own qualities, and the number of
the day had also to be considered. The numbers 3, 7, 10–13
were fortunate, while 4, 5, 6, 8, and 9 brought bad luck. The
number 2 in combination with the sign Rabbit was especially
unfortunate, and the figure 1 was usually neutral. In addition,
each of the 20 day-signs was consecrated to a god or goddess.
Quetzalcoatl, as befits a wind god, was lord of the sign Wind

and was therefore patron of the 13 days with which this sign appeared: Tlaloc was god of the sign Deer, and Xipe Totec of the sign Eagle.

There were more complications to follow. The day was divided into 13 hours and the night into 9 hours, each of which had its own deity and its own good or bad influence. Each of the calendar 'weeks' was also under the patronage of a divinity who was responsible for the period as a whole. Xipe Totec, for instance, ruled over the week beginning with One Dog, while the Water Goddess presided over week One Reed.

The soothsayers had also to consider the sign and number of the year, and to take account of the spatial orientation of the

81 Page from the Tonalamatl (Book of the Days) of the Codex Borbonicus, representing the 13-day period presided over by the goddess Tlazolteotl, Eater of Filth. The goddess, dressed in a flayed skin, is the principal figure in the main panel. The smaller divisions show the gods and symbols of the individual days and hours

days. The 20 day-signs were divided into four sets of five, and each group was assigned to one of the four cardinal points or 'directions' (82). These four quarters had their own colour symbolism and propensities for good or evil, and were themselves ruled over by the four creator gods:

East: colour red; god Xipe Totec. The region of light, and therefore of fertility and life.

North: colour black; god Tezcatlipoca. The region of the dead, associated with cold and barrenness. Unlucky.

West: colour white; god Quetzalcoatl. Land of women, and the place where the sun set. Associated with old age and declining powers. Unfortunate.

South: colour blue; god Huitzilopochtli. The symbol of the southern quarter was a rabbit, whose next leap nobody can anticipate. The influence of this direction was therefore uncertain or neutral.

The Calendar Round

The most important unit of time was a 52-year period, sometimes called the 'Calendar Round', which was arrived at by intermeshing the 260-day Almanac Year with the 365-day Solar one. Each of these cycles repeated itself endlessly throughout time, and any given day could therefore be expressed in terms of two quite different calendars. The problem was to discover a unit which had significance for both the Almanac and the Solar cycles, and the answer, which had been known in Mexico since before the time of Christ, was the 52-year period. The best way to follow the reasoning is to work out an example.

The year when Cortés landed in Mexico (1519 by our system) was 1 Reed in Aztec terminology. In other words, New Year's Day (Day 1 of the first month in the Solar Year) fell on the day 1 Reed of the Almanac Year, a combination which would not recur until 52 years had passed. This figure is reached by taking the least common multiple of 260 and 365. Both numbers can be divided by 5; 260 gives a quotient of 52, and 365 gives a quotient of 73. The least common multiple will therefore be $5 \times 52 \times 73$, which gives 18,980 days, or 52 years.

Employing the cog wheel analogy (pp. 165–166) we will have to imagine one wheel with 260 teeth (the days of the Almanac Year), and the other with 365 (one for each day of the Solar Year). If the machinery was started when 1 Reed of the Almanac

82 Page 1 of the Codex Fejervary Mayer. In the central panel is the Fire God, and in the trapeze-shaped sections are the gods of the four directions. At the four corners are the birds which carry the names of the year symbols. The border of the entire design gives the sequence of 13-day periods: at each corner or intersection is one of the 20 day-signs, and the dots between them indicate the 12 days which, with the preceding day-sign, make up a 13-day period

wheel was opposite Day 1 of the Solar wheel, the Almanac wheel would need to make 73 complete revolutions and the Solar wheel 52 before the same two cogs would meet again.

Any date, whether day or year, could be fixed in terms of its position in the 52-year cycle, but unfortunately the scribes who kept the historical records did not trouble to number the cycles individually. An event ascribed to the year 1 Reed could have taken place in 1519, 1467, 1415, or any other date which maintained the 52-year interval.

The longest unit of time was two Calendar Rounds, or 104 years. The Venus year has 584 days, with the result that five Venus cycles are the equivalent of eight Solar years. The 104-year period, which the Aztecs called 'one old age', was a unit of great calendrical significance, for at the start of it the Almanac, Solar, and Venus years all coincided.

The 52-year periods were named *xiuhmolpilli*, meaning 'bundle of years', or 'tying up of the years'. In the manuscripts the scribes employed two different glyphs to indicate this cycle, one a bundle of reeds tied together with a cord, the other a drawing of the fire-drill and baseboard which the priests used to kindle the flames for the New Fire Ceremony held at the end of every *xiuhmolpilli* (83).

Aztec creation myths foretold a time when the world would come to an end, when the stars and planets would turn into monsters which would devour all mankind, and when earthquakes would destroy the sun. This catastrophe was expected on the final day of a cycle, and the five 'hollow days' which ended the last year of the old cycle were therefore a time of crisis and deep uneasiness. No one could be sure that the sun would rise again and the world be safe for another 52 years. During the unfortunate days all fires were put out, people cleaned their homes, threw away their old garments, and smashed all their pottery to symbolize the end of the old cycle.

At nightfall on the final day, the priests dressed themselves in the costumes of the gods and marched in procession from the great temple in Tenochtitlán to an extinct volcanic cone, called the Hill of the Star, some seven miles outside the city. On its peak stood a temple which overlooked the whole of the Valley, and here the astronomer-priests stationed themselves, observing the progress of the star Alcyone and the constellation of the Pleiades. Below them a vast crowd watched and waited. Those who had to remain in the city went up onto the roofs of their houses and fixed their eyes on the mountain top, straining to catch a glimpse of the fire which was the sign that Alcyone had reached the meridian and that the sun would, after all, rise again the following day.

At the moment when the star reached the centre of the heavens, the priests on the hilltop seized a sacrificial victim and stretched him on his back over the altar. The fireboard was placed on his chest and, while all the assembly gave a great shout, the high priest of the Capulco quarter of Tenochtitlán took up the firestick and rotated it on the baseboard until the friction caused the wood to burst into flames. The captive's heart was torn out and thrown into the fire, while the priests tended the blaze until they had made a beacon which could be seen from every part of the Valley.

83 Making fire by rotating a stick against a fireboard

Runners from all the nearby towns thrust pinewood torches into the New Fire and hurried to relight the fires in every local temple. Once kindled, these sacred fires were not allowed to go out until the 52-year cycle ended. From the temples the New Fire was distributed to every household, making the night as bright as day.

On the morrow there were feasts and further sacrifices. To symbolize the start of a new cycle the people put on new clothes, replaced the broken pottery, whitewashed their homes, and even replaced their household idols with fresh ones. Mankind was saved, but the respite was only temporary. No one could tell whether this new cycle would not also be the last.

Sacrifice

The Mexican attitude towards human sacrifice had its roots in the creation myths already described. The sun, and hence the entire universe, owed its existence to the self-immolation of the gods, while man himself was not created until Quetzalcoatl had mingled his own blood with the bones collected from the land of the dead. The stability of the world depended on collaboration between gods and men, on the correct performance of the rites, and on the offering of blood both in recognition of the original act of creation and, on a more practical level, as nourishment for the Sun and all the other gods.

These beliefs were shared by captor and victim alike, and

between them grew up a kind of mystical kinship in which the blood link was through sacrifice rather than family descent.

And the captor might not eat of the flesh of his captive. He said: 'Shall I, then, eat my own flesh?' For when he took the captive he had said: 'He is as my beloved son.' And the captive had said: 'He is as my beloved father.' And yet he might eat of someone else's captive. (Sahagún's informants, describing the ceremonies of the second month.)

From the moment of his submission, the prisoner entered into a special relationship with his captor. In Mexican imagery, they were of one family and one flesh.

Human sacrifice became progressively more important in Mexican religion, but was probably not practised on a massive scale until the middle of the fifteenth century. After his victory over Azcapotzalco in 1428, Itzcoatl and his adviser, Tlacaelel, initiated a policy of conquest, encouraging the Aztecs to think of themselves as Huitzilopochtli's chosen people whose mission was to feed the sun, while at the same time increased military activity brought more and more captives to Tenochtitlán.

By 1487 the custom was well established. In that year the great temple of Huitzilopochtli was dedicated, and to mark the occasion 20,000 captives were slain. The kings of Tenochtitlán and Texcoco began the killing, and then handed over to the priests who worked continuously for four days until the last victim was dispatched. The captives stood in four lines which stretched for two miles through the streets of the city.

It is estimated that the Aztecs sacrificed 10,000–50,000 victims each year, mostly war captives, but also slaves and children who were obtained by purchase. Each town or village held its own ceremonies. In the feasts of the fourteenth calendar month (wrote Motolinía) 'they sacrificed, according to the size of the village, 20, 40, and even 50 or 60 people; in Mexico they sacrificed more than 100'. The heads of the victims were skewered in rows on wooden frameworks (35), and Andres de Tapia (who served under Cortés) counted the skulls on the rack which stood beside the main temple in Tenochtitlán: 'The writer and a certain Gonzalo de Umbria counted the cross sticks which were stretched from pole to pole, as I have described, and multiplying by five skulls per cross piece we found there to be 136,000 heads, without those of the towers.' The towers which he mentions were made of skulls cemented by lime mortar.

The most common offerings were fresh hearts, and human blood which the priests smeared on the images of the gods. The victim was spread-eagled breast upwards over a low stone block, and a priest grasped each of his limbs. A fifth priest held the head, while another used a flint or obsidian knife to open the captive's chest with a sideways stroke which cut through the ribs and breastbone (84 and 85). The heart was wrenched out, held up to the sun, then put aside in a wooden or stone vessel called an 'eagle dish' (86 and 87). The whole operation was

84 Human sacrifice
(Codex Florentino)

over in a few moments. Sometimes the victims fainted or had to be dragged struggling to the altar, but most of them died willingly, fortified by the knowledge that they would go straight to the paradise of the sun.

The act of sacrifice was the climax in a chain of ceremonies which varied according to the god who was being honoured. Each of the 18 months had its festival, and many of them were lengthy and elaborate affairs, full of the symbolism in which the Aztec mind delighted. The feast of Tezcatlipoca, for example, fell in the fifth month, but preparations began a year in advance when the priests chose an unblemished young captive to be the incarnation of the god on earth.

The youth was taught how to behave as a nobleman, and for a year he was revered as a lord and a living god. The priests taught him to play the flute, and he was given an entourage of eight attendants who went with him everywhere. His face was anointed with black paint, and he was dressed in costly garments with gold bracelets on his arms and golden bells on his legs. His time was spent in pleasure, and when he strolled through the city with tobacco tube in hand and with his neck garlanded with flowers all people did him homage.

Twenty days before the festival, the god-impersonator was married to four young women. His dress and hair style were changed to those of a war chief, and the last five days before the ceremony were passed in feasting, singing, and dancing in various parts of the city.

On the day of the sacrifice the young man, accompanied by his wives and by attendants who tried to console him, was taken in a canoe to a small temple on the lake shore. There the women took leave of him, and he walked to the temple steps, carrying the flutes which he had played during his year of office. At the foot of the pyramid his pages left him and, quite alone now, he slowly mounted the staircase, breaking one of the clay flutes at each step. Above him the priests were waiting, and when the young man reached the summit they seized him and tore out his heart. As soon as he had died, another captive was chosen to take his place as the incarnation of Tezcatlipoca for the year ahead.

The idea of a god-impersonator appears in many of the Aztec ceremonies. The festival of the eighth month was under the patronage of Xilonen, the goddess of young corn which at this time of the year was just beginning to ripen, and her part was taken by a slave girl who was decapitated to symbolize the gathering of the maize heads. In the eleventh month, the woman who impersonated the goddess of ripe maize suffered the same fate.

The ceremony in honour of the Fire God was one of the most gruesome. Prisoners were bound hand and foot, and a powder made from a plant of the hemp family was cast into their faces to act as an anaesthetic. Each prisoner was lifted on to the back of his captor, and the warriors began a dance around a great bonfire. Then, one by one, the dancers cast their victims into the blaze, but before death could intervene the priests dragged out the blistered and half-burned bodies with hooks and opened them up to remove the hearts.

Not all offerings involved death and sacrifice. At certain

85 Sacrificial knife with handle in the shape of an Eagle Knight

174

festivals the gods were presented with flowers and ears of maize, or with images made of wood and amaranth dough.

Most of the ceremonies included feasting and dancing as well as blood-letting, and there were many occasions for the people to work off surplus energy. In the tenth month, a pole some 150 feet high was set up and topped

86 Stone dish used in blood and heart sacrifices. Probably from Tenochtitlán

with an image made of amaranth dough. The young men scrambled to see who would be first up, and the winner was given a prize of jewellery and a mantle. In other months mock combats were held between Eagle and Jaguar knights, and between men and women, or priests and laymen. Some of these contests were sheer buffoonery and were filled with a carnival spirit, but those in connection with the festival of Tlaloc gave the priests licence to beat and rob anyone who interrupted their procession. There must have been plenty of opportunities for paying off personal scores, and there seems at times to have been some real antagonism between the classes.

Temples and priests

The great temple of Tenochtitlán has already been described (pp. 100–101), and its basic plan, with one or two shrines standing on top of a stepped pyramid, was repeated in hundreds of lesser buildings. Of the few which survive, the pyramid of Tenayuca is one of the most completely excavated, and archaeology has shown that it was remodelled or enlarged eight times during the Toltec, Chichimec, and Aztec periods. By the time of the Conquest the original pyramid had doubled in size, and the excavators found the earlier structures, nesting one inside the other like a set of Chinese boxes, still preserved within the body of the mound.

87 Stone dish from Tenochtitlán. The vessel is in the form of a jaguar, and was used as a receptacle for human hearts during sacrificial rites

The normal plan of both pyramids and temples was rectangular, but those dedicated to Ehécatl, the Wind God, were often round. This shape may have been chosen because it offered less resistance to the wind, and good examples can be seen at Tlatelolco and at Calixtlahuaca where a fine statue of Ehécatl (72), wearing his characteristic beak-shaped mask, was dug up in the corner of a platform built onto the front of the round pyramid.

At Malinalco is a unique group of temples, some of which were still unfinished when the Spaniards arrived. The buildings lie on a terraced slope, and many of the staircases, platforms, and wall-footings are cut into the natural rock. The most interesting structure is a circular temple entered through a doorway carved to resemble a serpent head with curved fangs and staring eyes—very similar, in fact, to the one described by Bernal Diaz in Tenochtitlán (pp. 101–102 and 90). The entrance was flanked by sculptured Eagle and Jaguar Knights, and inside was a semicircular stone bench carved with representations of eagles and an ocelot. In the centre of the floor was another eagle with its beak pointing through the doorway. The upper courses of the walls were of dressed stone, and there would originally have been a conical roof made of straw. In spite of its circular plan the presence of so many eagle and jaguar symbols suggests that the building was dedicated to the Sun, to whose service the knightly orders were vowed.

The gods were served by a specialist class of priests and priestesses. The Spanish chronicler, Torquemada, records that 5,000 people were employed at the Temple of Huitzilopochtli alone, and the figure for Tenochtitlán as a whole must have run into tens of thousands.

At the top of the religious hierarchy were the high priests of the two principal Aztec gods, Huitzilopochtli and Tlaloc,

88 Temple platforms at Calixtlahuaca. The round temple
is not shown

whose shrines stood side by side on top of the great pyramid. The
two priests were equal in status and were chosen for their
special sanctity, irrespective of lineage or family background.

They were assisted by a priest who acted as a sort of secretary-
general of the church. He took charge of the religious affairs
of Tenochtitlán and the subject provinces, and was also
superintendent-in-chief of the *calmecac* schools. Below him came
two lesser officials, one of whom looked after the day-to-day
running of the schools while the other was a consultant on all
matters of ritual and also acted as overseer of the religious
orders. The lowest administrative post was that of the *Ometochtzin*
(Two Rabbit) who was both priest of the Pulque God and chief
of the singers.

Of the ordinary clergy, those of the highest rank were
important dignitaries who had charge of the worship of individual gods. They were helped by lesser priests, the 'curates' of
the Aztec church, and below these, at the base of the ecclesi-
astical pyramid, came the temple novices, boy trainees from the
calmecac schools, who were not yet ordained and who did all the
odd jobs about the temples.

The life of a priest was neither comfortable nor easy. He was
not allowed to marry, and his time was governed by a routine
as strict as that of any Christian monastery. Four times during
the day and five times during the night he was required to pray
and offer incense in the temple. He fasted often, and further
mortified his flesh by blood-letting. There is a picture in the
Codex Mendoza of a priest setting off for the mountains to make

a blood-offering at night. He carries a ladle-shaped incense burner (89) in one hand and his incense pouch in the other; on his back hangs a gourd containing tobacco in the form of snuff or pellets to sustain him on the journey, and under his arm are the green branches which he will sprinkle with his blood and leave on the altar. He is followed at a respectful distance by a novitiate carrying cactus spines for the blood-letting.

Some priests became experts in one or other branch of learning, in particular astrology, divination, and calendrics. The priests were the nation's time-keepers, and it was one of their duties to parade through the streets of Tenochtitlán in the early mornings rousing the citizens from their beds by a chorus of shell trumpets. Other priests specialized in music. They worked under the direction of the *Ometochtzin* and his assistant (The Lord of the House of Flutes) in the school where sacred music was taught, and in the codices we can see them chanting and practising their instruments.

They could also hold secular offices. Priests became judges or even commanders of troops, and, like the battling bishops of medieval Europe, they set off for the fray accompanied by novices who served them as squires. They fought alongside the other warriors and, like them, took prisoners, were promoted, and received insignia if they distinguished themselves (96). During their nocturnal journeys the priests also acted as sentries.

Behind the scenes the priesthood was able to influence secular life through control of the *calmecac* schools in which all Aztec leaders were educated. As the guardians of knowledge and traditions, and as members of a class whose duty it was to ascertain the will of the gods and to interpret it here on earth, the priests were a political force to be reckoned with.

Even their appearance commanded respect. Their bodies were painted black, and their usual costume was a black or dark green mantle reaching to the feet. As a macabre touch these cloaks were

89 Incense-burner of Cholula pottery

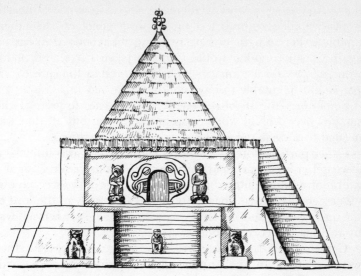

90 Reconstruction of the round temple at Malinalco

occasionally embroidered with human skulls and bones. Hair was never cut, washed, or combed, and as a result of service in the temple it soon became matted with blood. A priest, with his emaciated body, his ear-lobes ragged from blood-letting, and his smell compounded of stale blood, incense, and decaying flesh, represented both the best and the worst in Aztec religion.

Superstition and sorcery

We might expect that a people obsessed with astrology and fortune-telling would have a great number of popular superstitions; after all, many of us today feel uneasy if we spill salt, walk under a ladder, or break a mirror! Aztec superstitions were every bit as irrational as our own, and some of them were not dissimilar. When a child lost one of his milk teeth the mother dropped the tooth into a mouse hole, for without this precaution the second tooth would not grow. When a person sneezed, he said, 'Somebody is talking about me', just as we occasionally say the same thing when our ears burn. The Aztecs had a fund of such beliefs. They thought, for example, that a girl who ate her meal standing up would be married a long way from home, that a man who accidentally kicked one of the hearth stones would get numb feet on the battlefield and would be unable either to fight or run away, that anybody who leaned against a square pillar would grow up to be a liar, and that a woman who ate a tamale which had stuck to the side of the pot would be unable to have children.

Sometimes the ill effect could be avoided. A person who stepped over a child would stop him growing, but all that was needed to reverse the spell was to step back again.

Other portents foretold sickness and death. It was unlucky if a weasel crossed one's path, if the roof beams creaked, or if a rabbit or a skunk entered the house. The cry of the screech owl was especially feared, for this bird was the envoy of the lord of the underworld, and the only way a man could save himself was by reciting the correct counter-spell.

Comets or earthquakes were of such importance that they were recorded in the annals. Shortly before the Spaniards arrived all the signs foretold a great national disaster. Comets appeared in the heavens; the temple of Huitzilopochtli caught fire of its own accord and could not be extinguished; on a windless day the waters of the lake rose up and flooded the city; and (most frightening of all) a phantom woman was heard weeping in the streets at night, crying out, 'O my beloved sons, now we are at the point of going. My beloved sons, whither shall I take you?'

Night was always a dangerous time, for demons walked in the hours of darkness. Tezcatlipoca, god of the wizards, took many forms, appearing as a shrouded corpse, or a bundle of ashes which groaned as it billowed along, or as a headless man with his chest and belly broken open (91). Anyone bold enough to seize this spectre and tear out its heart could demand a reward for giving it back, but there is no record of anyone having made the attempt. The only safe thing to do after seeing this apparition or one of the other ghostly beings (like the female goblins which haunted the dung heaps, or the severed head which leaped from the shadows) was to run home and put an obsidian knife into a bowl of water so that the demon, when it came to look at its reflection in the bowl, would be frightened away.

In this sort of atmosphere sorcery flourished. Official religion had its astrologers, but they should not be confused with the men and women who practised magic for profit. Many of these people were professional conjurers and quacks who astonished simple folks by performing such tricks as roasting maize on an ordinary piece of cloth without the aid of fire. The Huastecs were credited with special powers. It was said that a Huastec magician could create from nothing a spring with live fishes swimming in its waters, and could even resurrect himself after being cut into pieces— although, like the Indian rope trick, this performance was often talked about but never seen.

91 A traveller meets a spectre at night (Codex Florentino)

Fortunes were told by throwing grains of maize into a bowl of water. If the grains sank to the bottom the future would be lucky, but if some of them floated they indicated misfortune and death. The fortune-teller could control the result by selecting the grain beforehand, since good grain will always sink while rotten grain will stay on the surface. Other diviners worked by throwing grains onto a mat, and if most of the grains fell face-upwards it was taken as a sign of good fortune.

People born on the days 3 Alligator and 1 Wind were predisposed towards black magic, and all days which bore the number 9 were especially favourable for their activities. These sorcerers were the most feared of all. They had the power to change themselves into animals, could send wasting diseases (hence their name 'heart-eaters'), and could drive a person mad by putting the evil eye on him. They offered their gifts for hire, and would do any wickedness for a fee. Their most powerful charm was the forearm of a woman who had died in childbirth, and bands of sorcerers armed with one of these would arrive at a house, send all the occupants to sleep, and rob the building at their leisure. If this really did happen—and Sahagún's informants seemed convinced that it did—terror rather than any sort of mass hypnotism seems to have been the magicians' weapon, for we read that the householders swooned with fear so that they could neither move nor cry out.

Medicine

It is difficult to separate medicine from religion and magic. The Aztec *tititl*, a man or woman skilled in healing, combined the functions of a doctor with those of a sorcerer and magician, and his remedies were a hotch-potch of religious incantations, genuine herbal knowledge, faith-healing, and, at times, sheer quackery.

When a person fell ill the healer was called in to give a diagnosis. This was not a simple matter, for although the nature of the disease could be recognized by observing the symptoms, the true cause of the malady might lie outside the patient's body altogether. Sickness could be sent by the gods, either out of sheer malignancy or as a punishment for some breach of ritual, such as eating during a public fast. The *ciuapipiltin*, the souls of women who had died in childbirth (p. 71) were thought to haunt crossroads on certain unlucky dates and to cause paralysis in young children to whom they appeared. Other diseases, such as leprosy, dropsy, gout, swellings, and ulcers, came from Tlaloc and were borne on the cold winds which came from the hills where the mountain gods, the *Tlaloque*, lived. Xipe Totec presided over skin disorders and eye troubles, while Amimitl was responsible for coughs and dysentery.

Diseases like these, caused by the displeasure of the gods, could be avoided by proper observance of the rites and by wearing protective amulets. The god who sent the disease could be appeased by repentance or offerings, and some gods were actively helpful in healing illness. Sick children, for example, were cured by drinking water from jars kept in the temple of Ixtlilton.

Some ailments were the result of magic by which a foreign, disease-causing object was introduced into the body of the sufferer. The best cure for witchcraft was to employ a sorcerer of one's own to find and get rid of the irritant, and also to discover the name of the enemy responsible for the disease. Certain classes of healing women were known as *tetlacuicuilique* (they who draw out stones), or *teixocuilanque* (those who draw out worms from the eyes). After the appropriate invocations, the healer would rub her hands over the tender spot, or apply suction to the seat of the pain, and then produce a worm or some small object of paper, flint, or obsidian, which she pretended to have extracted from the patient's body.

To find out which god or enemy had sent the disease, the healers resorted to divination. Sometimes a bundle of thin cords was thrown on the ground and the diagnosis determined by the pattern: if the cords remained tangled it was a bad sign and foretold death, but if one or more of the cords fell apart from the others it meant that the patient would recover. Often drugs were administered to the patient or taken by the healer. The usual drugs were *peyotl* and *ololiuhqui*, both of which cause visions and hallucinations, and in his dreams and babblings the person would reveal the cause of the malady, naming the god whose displeasure was responsible or the enemy whose witchcraft had sent the illness. Sick children were held over a bowl of water which acted as a mirror. The healer invoked the water goddess and examined the child's reflection in the water. If the sufferer's face appeared darkened or shadowy, it meant that the 'soul' or 'vital breath' had been stolen away.

After the diagnosis came the treatment. Spells, prayers, and incantations were part of the cure, and the healers used a secret and esoteric language to impress the patients. Blood was called 'red woman'; pains were called 'serpents' and were assigned to the four cardinal points with their characteristic colours. The following incantation was recited over a patient with chest sickness:

Come, you the five *tonalli* [a magical term for the healer's fingers]. I the priest, I the lord of spells, I seek the green pain, the tawny pain. Where is it hidden? Enchanted medicine, I say to you, I the lord of spells, that I wish to heal this sick flesh. So you must go to the seven caves [the lungs]. Do not touch the yellow heart, enchanted medicine. I expel from this place the green pain, the tawny pain. Come, you the nine winds, expel the green pain, the tawny pain.

Many of the remedies (like the morning dew dropped into the nostrils of children who snuffled) had a purely magical value, and tobacco smoke and copal incense were used to purify the room in which the healing took place.

The Aztecs suffered from many of the diseases endemic in rural Mexico today, especially intestinal disorders, dysentery, and parasitic infections. Other common complaints were fevers, rheumatism, and skin troubles ranging from leprosy and ring-worm to minor ailments like scabs, boils, and dandruff. Lice were common enough to inspire the following riddle:

Q. What is it that is seized in a black forest and dies on a white stone slab?
A. It is a louse that we take from our head, put on our nail and then kill.

Cataract and squinting were prominent among eye diseases. The mortality rate among children was high, and probably not more than half of them survived beyond early infancy. In compensation, a number of diseases (including measles, typhoid, smallpox, yellow fever, and malaria) were absent from Mexico until introduced by the Spaniards.

The texts make it clear that the more intelligent Aztecs distinguished between doctors who used well-tried remedies and the quacks who traded on popular credulity. Not all Aztec medicine depended on prayers and magical formulae. The virtues of the steam bath were recognized for curing stiffness, inducing labour in pregnant women, sweating out coughs and chills, and even (after drinking an infusion of herbs) for clearing a blotchy complexion. Doctors seem to have realized that external ailments like pustules and swollen faces could be due to internal disturbances, and the treatment included purging as well as dressing with powdered herbs. For a cough the patient had first to take an emetic, followed by an infusion of herbs in water or maguey wine, and then a carefully regulated diet:

he is to drink boiled chili-water, or atole with yellow chili and honey. He will not drink cold water. He will abstain from choco-late, fruit, yellow maguey wine. He will avoid the cold, the chill; he will cover himself well. Also the sweat bath will help him. There in the sweat bath he will inhale the hot air.   (Sahagún)

Aztec healers had discovered the therapeutic properties of about 1,200 plants, some of which are still unidentified, while others—for example, valerian (a mild stimulant), pennyroyal (inhaled for catarrh), jalap (a purgative), and the plant called *ciuapatli* (*Montanoa tomentosa*, used to accelerate childbirth)— have been tested scientifically and shown to possess the qualities which the Mexicans attributed to them. There were herbal remedies to stop bleeding, to bring down the temperature during fever, to cure disorders of the stomach and bowels, to act against fits, and to heal a multitude of skin complaints. Minor sores were cured by a poultice of squashed black beetles.

For hoarseness, 'many times the throat is massaged with liquid rubber. And bee honey is to be drunk, and many times, by way of the nose, bee honey or thickened maguey syrup will drop into the throat' (Sahagún). Protruding tongues were massaged with rubber sap, and ulcers inside the ear were treated with a few drops of the same substance. Animal flesh could also have curative properties; swollen faces, for instance, were healed by repeated purging followed by a meal of roast or fried chameleon.

Inflamed throats, stiff necks, sprains, and similar ailments, were treated by massage, often in conjunction with a steam bath and a poultice of cooked herbs to reduce the swelling. If these measures did not ease the pressure, the healer used an obsidian blade to lance the swelling itself or to open a nearby blood vessel. Dislocated limbs were manipulated back into place and broken limbs were splinted until the bone knitted together.

Some attempt was made to avoid dental trouble. People were warned against eating very hot or very cold food, and especially against drinking cold water immediately after a hot meal, before the teeth had had time to cool. It was realized that food particles between the teeth caused them to decay, and so the doctors advised regular cleaning. Salt and powdered charcoal were used as a polish, and tartar was carefully scraped off with a metal tool. For those unlucky enough to develop a tooth infection,

> as its cure, pine resin mixed with ground *conyayaoal* worms is placed as a poultice over the surface. And one presses a heated chili upon the tooth, and one presses salt upon the tooth. And the gums are pricked, and the herb *tlalcacauatl* is applied on the tooth. If nothing reduces the infection, the tooth is extracted; salt is inserted into the cavity. (Sahagún)

For a people whose religion demanded large-scale human sacrifice the Mexicans showed little interest in surgery and anatomy. Boils, abscesses, tumours, and cysts were lanced, and doctors resorted to bleeding as part of the cure for headaches, worms in the eyelids, swollen tongues, and inflamed joints. Flesh wounds, which must have been common in such a warlike society, were sewn up, using hair as a suture.

9

War

War for the Aztecs was both an economic and a psychological necessity. Mexican politics were based on power rather than morality; the stronger states bullied or annexed the weaker ones, and the only guarantee of independence was a strong army. For the dominant nations there were good pickings to be had, and at the time of the Conquest the Aztecs were living parasitically on the tribute from subject provinces. So many people had been drawn into the non-productive classes that Tenochtitlán had long since outgrown its own resources and had become dependent on extortion for its very existence as an imperial city.

Temperamentally, too, the Aztecs were unfitted for peaceful life. In the days of their early military successes they had come to believe that their destiny was to conquer, an attitude which Mexican leaders, with an eye on the political and economic advantages, had been careful to encourage. This belligerence had to have its outlet: every young man wanted his chance to excel.

The Aztecs felt themselves a chosen people in a religious as well as a military sense. Their mission was to nourish the gods with the human blood which alone could sustain them in the battle against the forces of darkness, and war took on a religious significance, becoming an act of worship in itself. Wars were fought as much to obtain prisoners for sacrifice as to gain land or booty, and during peaceful interludes, when victims were in short supply, the armies engaged in the 'War of Flowers', a ceremonial combat in which the warriors of the Triple Alliance did battle with those of Tlaxcala, Cholula, and Uexotzinco. The aim on both sides was to take as many captives as possible, and once the priests judged that enough victims had been taken to satisfy the needs of the gods, the 'War' was called off and the armies returned peacefully home.

Mexican warfare, whether in earnest or not, never quite lost this ceremonial character.

The army, its equipment and weapons

A large standing army was unnecessary because every Aztec youth had learned to handle weapons as part of his school training. From the age of 15 (or 20 according to some authorities) a young man was liable for military service and indeed was anxious to go to war. Apart from the mystique attached to a soldier's life, success on the battlefield opened the way to higher honours and was one of the few ways in which a man of humble origin could rise in the world. Warriors received no pay, but those who distinguished themselves were rewarded by gifts of clothing and slaves, or of private estates with peasants to work on the land. From the ranks of the successful warriors were chosen the captains, directors of schools, tax gatherers, judges, and a host of minor officials. Although noble birth was an advantage, promotion was by merit, and any soldier who managed to capture four prisoners gained automatic entry into the ruling class. It was possible for an exceptional man to work his way up from common soldier to a rank only one grade below that of commander-in-chief.

The smallest unit in the army was the squad of 20 men, and these were combined into larger groupings of 200, 400, and 800 warriors, commanded at each level by regular officers who were often members of the knightly orders of the Eagle, the Jaguar, and the Arrow. Each of the 20 clans of Tenochtitlán provided a contingent of soldiers, and the structure of the army reflected that of the city itself with the clans of a given quarter fighting side by side in the same division.

The four divisional commanders were important men who were usually blood relations of the Emperor and were charged with civil as well as military duties. All four acted as counsellors to the monarch, and the ruler's successor was often chosen from among them. Montezuma II, for example, held the position during the reign of his father, Ahuítzotl, as did Montezuma I when his cousin, Itzcoatl, was king.

By virtue of his office the ruler was both head of the Tenochtitlán army and commander-in-chief of the forces of the Aztec confederation. Rulers often led their armies in person, but in times of continuous warfare the command was some-times delegated to a war chief who held office for a single campaign.

Each city or tribe under Allied control could muster an army of its own, and it has been estimated that, drawing on all the home provinces, the Alliance could put 100,000 men into the field. Mexican chronicles refer to armies of anything from 20,000 to 200,000 warriors divided into tribal contingents led by their own officers, but under the supreme command of Tenochtitlán.

The troops did not wear uniform. Each soldier dressed as he thought fit, putting on all the trappings to which his rank and military record entitled him, so that a warrior's status was obvious at once from his costume, insignia, and even hair style. A Jaguar Knight wore the battledress of his order (a tightly fitting ocelot skin which covered his trunk and limbs, and was pulled up over the head so that his face showed through the animal's open jaws) (77), and an Eagle Knight could be recognized by a helmet shaped like the head of an eagle with a gaping beak (85). Lesser captains wore wooden or leather helmets, carved into all sorts of fantastic shapes and decorated with feather crests or devices made from cloth and paper (4).

Leaders of regiments or city contingents carried banners which were attached to their backs by means of shoulder harnesses which left the arms free for action. These

92 Shield decorated with a panel of feather mosaic forming the name-glyph of King Ahuítzotl. Probably obtained by Cortés from Montezuma

standards were made from feathers or from reeds and paper spread over a wooden frame, and each force had its own distinctive emblem which served as a rallying point during the battle. The Tlaxcalan device was a white heron with outspread wings, while Tepetipac had a wolf with arrows, and Ocotelolco a green bird perched on a rock.

93 Man using spear-thrower and dart

Loose garments were an encumbrance on the battlefield, so the warriors discarded their cloaks in favour of body armour made from quilted cotton soaked in brine. The usual form was a tight-fitting combination suit, about two fingers thick, with corselet and knee-length trousers made in one piece, and the upper part laced at the back so that it had no dangling bits which an enemy could seize (4 and 96). Against lances and arrows it was so effective that the Spaniards often wore it in preference to their own steel armour which was heavy and hot to wear. The Mexicans indulged their love of display by ornamenting these cotton suits with heraldic devices, and on top of them soldiers of noble birth sometimes wore cuirasses made of gold plates.

The usual type of shield was a round buckler, 20–30 inches in diameter. One surviving example (probably from a consignment which Cortés sent to Europe) is made of rods laid side by side and held in place by threads of twisted cotton. Lying diagonally across these are heavier slats to which the hand and arm grips are attached, and the shield is faced with leather decorated with feather mosaic stuck onto a bark-paper backing. Other shields were made of wood inlaid with gold or turquoise mosaic. The shields of the common soldiers were plain, but those of the captains bore personal emblems and insignia, while the shield of the commander carried his personal hieroglyph or the name of his people (92). Also in use were larger shields (probably made of leather or of wooden slats), which protected the body from head to foot and could be rolled up when not in use.

Long-range weapons were the javelin, bow, and sling. The javelin was a lightweight throwing-spear with a fire-hardened tip or a point made of chipped obsidian, and it was propelled by means of an *atlatl* (spear-thrower), a device which gave added range by artificially lengthening the thrower's arm (93). The spear-thrower consisted of a flat piece of wood, between one and two feet in length, with a groove down the centre in which the shaft of the javelin rested. One end of the *atlatl* was provided with a peg which engaged with the butt of the spear, and at the other end were finger-grips, sometimes in the form of loops made out of pieces of shell (94). Some javelins had more than one point and were occasionally provided with cords for retrieval.

Bows were rarely more than five feet long, and arrows were, either fire-hardened at the ends or else were tipped with bone or obsidian points.

Slings made of plaited cotton threw stones the size of eggs, and were the favourite weapon of the Matlatzinca who wore them tied around their heads when not required.

At close quarters the most deadly weapon was a kind of two-handed sword, consisting of a massive hardwood blade about a yard long with razor-sharp blades of obsidian set in grooves along the edges (77). This sword-club inflicted terrible wounds. It could decapitate a horse, and Díaz comments that it cut better than Spanish swords and was so sharp that an Indian could shave his head with it. The edge was soon lost, however, and the obsidian blades needed frequent replacement.

Lances, or thrusting spears, were anything from six to ten feet long, and in extreme cases the business end was a five-foot blade set with fragments of obsidian along the edges. Other examples were of more normal proportions and had heads of chipped obsidian or flint.

Less common weapons were heavy, knob-headed wooden clubs, and a kind of hatchet with a copper blade set into a thick shaft shaped like a policeman's truncheon.

The conduct of war

The Aztecs used war as the main instrument of their foreign policy, both defensive and offensive. The Empire was held together by force, and troops were sent to any city which failed to send its tribute or which attempted to leave the confederation. Outside the Empire, refusal to trade with the Mexicans, or mal-treatment of Aztec merchants, were con-

94 Wooden spear-thrower with finger-grips made of shell. The back is carved in relief (see fig. 95)

sidered acts of war, and, as we have seen, traders were sometimes encouraged to behave provocatively in the hope of causing an incident which might serve as a pretext for invasion. When the Aztecs had designs against a friendly state they became extra-ordinarily sensitive, taking offence where none was intended and looking for an insult which they could use as an excuse to declare war.

Attempts were made to frighten weaker states into sub-mission. The Aztecs realized that a destroyed city could not be expected to yield much tribute, and their aim was therefore to achieve the political objectives without having to fight. The talks were conducted with politeness and ceremony. First of all the ambassadors of Tenochtitlán spoke to the council of the 'enemy' city, inviting it to join the Mexican confederation and to share in the benefits of Mexican 'protection'. It was requested that Huitzilopochtli should be admitted to the temple on the same terms as the principal local god, and that normal commercial relations should be allowed. 'Of course', the envoys said, 'the city would keep its own chief and its own gods and customs. All that was required was a "treaty of friendship" [i.e. an acknowledgment of Mexican supremacy and the abandonment of an independent foreign policy], an assurance of free trade and, purely as a token of goodwill, a

95 Carved and gilt design on the back of a wooden spear-thrower

small present of gold, cotton, or precious stones for the rulers of the three allied states. Since this gift was to be a voluntary contribution, the city would be allowed to use its own discretion as to the size of the donation. No tax-gatherers or officials would be sent. . . .'

And so it went on; the words were courteous, the threat only implied. The language of diplomacy has not changed much— nor has the protection racket! As a parting gesture, 'so that it might never be said that they had been defeated by treachery', the ambassadors handed out a symbolic offering of swords and shields to the members of the council and then withdrew from the city for 20 days to allow their message to sink in.

If after that time the city had not given way, the envoys of Texcoco arrived. Their words were blunter. They pointed out that the local ruler would be put to death if he persisted in his obstinacy, and that his warriors would be taken and sacrificed. If, on the other hand, the city accepted the friendship of the Alliance its people would only be required to make a small gift every year. In the case of a refusal the Texcocans ceremonially anointed the chief's head with a liquid which would give him strength in battle, and fixed on his brow a tuft of feathers set in a band of red leather. More weapons were given out, and the ambassadors went away for another 20 days.

Finally, the representatives of Tlacopan went to the city and tried to undermine its ruler's authority by appealing directly to the townspeople, making it clear that a final refusal would mean war in which many would be killed or enslaved, the city and its lands ravaged, and the defeated state treated not as a friendly subordinate but as a vassal to be squeezed for all it was worth. Then followed the usual gift of weapons and a pause of 20 days.

If these threats proved ineffective the city was considered to be at war with the Alliance, but to preserve the fiction of legality the council of Tenochtitlán was allowed to debate the subject. The ruler, however, had the final word:

> But if it was a trivial cause, twice or thrice they advised against war, saying that there was no cause for it, and sometimes the ruler took their advice. But if he summoned them again and again, and insisted on war, they yielded to his importunities out of the respect they bore him, saying they would do his will, for they had told him their opinion and disclaimed responsibility in the matter. (Zorita)

Subjects and allies along the invasion route were warned to have their soldiers ready and to provide their share of provisions and carriers. The priests consulted the divine almanac to discover a lucky day to begin the war, and when the moment arrived a priest in the costume of Pay-nal, the messenger of

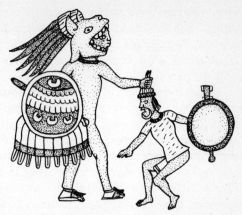

96 Warrior priest taking a captive

Huitzilopochtli, danced through the streets of Tenochtitlán with a rattle and a shield, calling out the warriors. The great war drum began to sound, and within an hour or so the army was mustered in front of the main temple.

When the army was on the move, the captains and scouts went ahead, closely followed by the priests bearing images of the gods. Behind them marched the tribal contingents, first the army of Tenochtitlán and then, in order, the forces of Texcoco, Tlacopan, and the levies from the provinces. To avoid congestion on the road each group remained a day's march behind the preceding one. The fighting men were accompanied by a host of auxiliaries: engineers whose job it was to construct ladders, bridges and water-tanks, women to do the cooking, and porters to carry the stores.

It was always a problem to keep a slow-moving infantry force supplied, especially during the later years of the Alliance when the wars were fought hundreds of miles from the capital. Since much of the route lay through friendly territory the troops could not be allowed to loot or forage for themselves, and any soldier who broke ranks or molested a civilian was executed. Advance parties made caches of food along the road, but the armies relied most of all on contributions from the cities through which they passed.

Because of the difficulty of keeping troops in the field for a long time, campaigns tended to be brief and a single battle was usually decisive. For the same reason prolonged sieges were rare, although the Tlaxcalans enclosed their territory by a stone wall which was described as 20 feet wide and 9 feet high with a wooden breastwork on top. At the gateways the wall was doubled for a distance of about 40 yards to leave a passageway only 10 paces wide between the two sections.

Battles began with a great deal of noise as each army tried to intimidate the other by shouting insults, clashing weapons, whistling, and beating drums. Then, at a signal from the commander's trumpet, the archers and slingers discharged their weapons at the enemy, the spearmen hurled their javelins, and the two armies rushed at each other in hand-to-hand combat. On the field the captains gave orders to their troops by means of gestures, drum beats, or blasts on clay whistles, while the war chief kept overall control, withdrawing tired squadrons and replacing them by fresh warriors from the reserve. Tactics were simple and consisted of attempts to outflank the enemy or to attack him from two sides at once. Sometimes an army would feign retreat, only to lead the pursuers into an ambush; another ruse was to dig camouflaged holes in which soldiers would hide until they could spring out on the unsuspecting enemy.

More often, however, the battle was a free-for-all in which ferocity and weight of numbers were the deciding factors. Victory was acknowledged when one side captured the opposing commander and seized his standard, or when the attackers captured the town's main temple and set fire to its shrine. In the manuscripts the glyph for defeat is a blazing temple transfixed by a spear.

Casualties were smaller than one might expect. Battles were usually short and sharp, and the object was not to kill the enemy outright but to take as many prisoners as possible. A warrior gained no glory by slaying an opponent, but was rewarded in proportion to the number of captives he had taken. The Aztecs ranked their foes according to fighting ability: Huastecs were considered poor stuff, and no matter how many of them a soldier captured he gained little credit for it, but if he managed to seize a single warrior of Atlixco or Uexotzinco he could be sure of promotion and a hero's welcome on his return.

The Aztecs' death-or-glory view of war shows in their attitude towards captivity. A captured Mexican was expected to face death without flinching. Honour demanded that he should not try to escape, and any nobleman who fled and returned to his own people was put to death, for (says Zorita) 'they said that since he had not been man enough to resist and die in battle he should have died a prisoner, for this was more honourable than to return home as a fugitive'.

When the battle was over, the dead were counted and the wounded treated by the surgeons. The first captives had already been sacrificed on the battlefield, but the rest were put into wooden cages to be taken back to the Allied cities. Scribes were in attendance to count the prisoners taken by each contingent, and a military court was set up to resolve any disputes.

Meanwhile a runner set off to bring news of the result to Tenochtitlán. If his tidings were bad the messenger entered the city in silence with his hair loose over his face, but if he had a victory to announce he bound up his hair and entered joyfully, brandishing his weapons, to be welcomed with flowers, incense, and the sound of trumpets. Other messengers visited the families of those who had died.

After the battle the adversaries negotiated peace terms. In the words of Jacques Soustelle, 'according to the Indian conception of it, the original institution of tribute was based upon a true contract, a contract of redemption. The conqueror had unlimited rights over the conquered, but the victorious city agreed to give up some of them in exchange for a solemn undertaking.' The quantity of tribute was fixed after hard bargaining between the two sides, the victors demanding an exorbitant amount of land or goods and threatening to renew the fighting, while the losers emphasized the poverty of their city and its inability to pay. Once agreement had been reached, the defeated city was given a formal warning against breaking the treaty. 'See to it that you fulfil and keep the agreement; in some future time do not say that this is not what you agreed to, nor claim that you made these promises because of fraud and deceit' (Tezozomoc, *Crónica mexïcana*). Under the terms of the Triple Alliance all gains of land or tribute were divided into five shares, two each for Tenochtitlán and Texcoco, and one for Tlacopan.

10

The Spanish Conquest

On Good Friday 1519 Cortés and his 600 Spanish adventurers landed on the Pacific coast of Mexico. On 13 August 1521, Tenochtitlán finally surrendered. The story of the Conquest has been told many times by men who took part in it and by historians using early Spanish sources, but these men, naturally enough, saw the Conquest through Spanish eyes, or at least judged it by European standards. To the Indians it appeared in a very different light.

The following section tells the story of the Conquest from the Aztec point of view and is based primarily on native Mexican accounts.

The Conquest as the Aztecs saw it

During the two years which preceded the Conquest there were signs that everything was not well in Mexico. Comets, sudden and inexplicable fires, floods, and deformed births all foretold disaster, until eventually Montezuma, who had a deep interest in magic and astrology, began to feel uneasy. Even his sooth-sayers were unable to interpret the omens. It was at this time that he challenged the ruler of Texcoco to a ball-game to test the prophecy that strangers would come to rule in Tenochtitlán (pp. 43–44), and when Montezuma lost the match he began to worry for his throne. He became still more demoralized when a messenger from the Gulf Coast arrived at Tenochtitlán with news of a strange 'hill' which moved upon the waters. The king sent envoys to confirm this information, and they returned with tales of 'floating towers' (the Spaniards' ships), of men with long yellow beards and complexions as white as chalk, and of 'deer' (horses) which carried these strange beings wherever they wanted to go. These strangers, the envoys reported, wore armour, had savage dogs with burning yellow eyes, and owned a fearsome machine (a cannon) which fired a thing like a ball of stone out of its entrails to the accompaniment of flames and a pestilential smell.

These marvels seemed not to belong to the world of men at all, and Montezuma began to fear that the newcomers were gods. The legend of Quetzalcoatl (p. 16)

97 The meeting of Cortés and Montezuma. In the foreground are the presents brought by the Aztecs (Lienzo de Tlaxcala)

was never very far from his mind, and in these bearded, fair-skinned and powerful beings he saw the god returning with his followers to claim the kingdom as he had promised in the days when the Toltecs ruled over Mexico. To make matters worse, 1519 was year One Reed in the Aztec calendar—and Ce Acatl (One Reed) was one of the sacred names of Quetzalcoatl.

These uncertainties go a long way towards explaining Montezuma's irresolute conduct. Mexican histories tell us that the king slept badly, had dreams and visions, and even contemplated flight. He sent the strangers costly gifts, including costumes and regalia of Quetzalcoatl. The messengers also carried food and drink for Quetzalcoatl/Cortés, though they must have been rather unnerved by Montezuma's parting words, 'If, by any chance, he does not like the food that you give him and is desirous of devouring human beings and wishes to eat you, allow yourselves to be eaten. I assure you that I will fulfil all my promises regarding your wives, children, and relatives.' The messengers returned uneaten, but their reports brought the king no peace of mind.

At the same time as he honoured the newcomers as gods, Montezuma made half-hearted efforts to keep them away from Tenochtitlán. He sent sorcerers to cast spells and, when these

failed, sent a guide to lead the Spaniards by a dangerous route
in the hope that they would fall over a precipice and be killed.
The strangers were immune to treachery as well as magic, and
the luckless Montezuma was still unable to decide whether he
had men or gods to deal with.

In the meantime the Spaniards continued their march towards Tenochtitlán. The Tlaxcalans, hereditary enemies of the
Aztecs, put the intruders to a more practical test and, having
been defeated in battle, allied themselves with Cortés. Other
tribes joined them, and the part played by these native allies
should not be underestimated. Tlaxcala provided a base in
friendly territory, and the Tlaxcalans kept the Spaniards supplied with provisions, porters, and workmen. The tiny Spanish
force, with iron armour, steel swords, muskets, and horses,
provided an élite corps which was supported by a host of Indian
auxiliaries and allies.

The invaders marched inland, took the city of Cholula, and
crossed over the pass leading into the Valley of Mexico. On
instructions from Montezuma, the Spaniards were welcomed at
Texcoco and eventually, on 8 November 1519, were allowed into
the capital itself without ever having fought an Aztec army (97).
The Spanish troops were lodged in the city, and Montezuma
permitted himself to be taken as hostage. Indian accounts of
Spanish conduct at this time are uncomplimentary but probably
not far from the truth, especially in their description of the
Spaniards' lust for treasure: 'They picked up the gold and
fingered it like monkeys: they seemed transported by joy, as
if their hearts were illuminated and made new . . . they
hungered like pigs for that gold.'

For a while the inhabitants swallowed their resentment and
put up with the intruders, but this precarious truce came to an
end while Cortés was away from Tenochtitlán. The Mexicans
had assembled peacefully to celebrate the festival of Huitzilopochtli, but Alvarado (Cortés' deputy), not trusting the crowd
in the temple precinct, ordered his men to fall on the Indians
without warning. After this massacre the Aztecs had no illusions
left. The people of the city rose against the Spaniards and
besieged them in their palace, but made a tactical blunder by
allowing Cortés to return with reinforcements and join his men
in their quarters. Even so, the invaders were in a desperate
situation, and after four days of harassment Cortés decided to

lead his troops out of the city, secretly and by night. While the column was filing along the causeway to the mainland it was seen by a woman drawing water, and when the Aztecs attacked again, harrying the fugitives by both land and water, the retreat became a rout. Only a quarter of the Spanish army escaped, but the survivors were not pursued and managed to regroup on the lake shore.

The first campaign had ended in victory for the Mexicans. During the siege, Montezuma was killed and was succeeded by Cuitlahuac and then, when the latter died of smallpox a few months later, by Cuauhtemoc, a man of great courage and resolution who led the Mexican resistance in its final stages.

The Spaniards returned with fresh troops, this time prepared for a long campaign. To ensure command of the lake Cortés had 12 brigantines constructed, and these, fitted with cannon, kept the lake free from Mexican canoes. The aqueduct was broken, thus depriving the Aztecs of fresh water, and by effectively controlling the causeways which were the only links with the mainland, the Spaniards were able to prevent any food reaching Tenochtitlán. Even the Texcocans turned against the Aztecs and joined forces with Cortés. Little by little the Spaniards advanced, pulling down houses to give the cavalry room to manœuvre and using the debris to fill the gaps in the causeways.

The siege lasted 80 days, and Ixtlilxochitl estimates that 240,000 people died in Tenochtitlán, some from wounds, others from disease and starvation. The city was completely without food: the inhabitants ate anything they could lay hands on— lizards, small birds, weeds and the bitter grasses of the lakeside, even deer skins and bits of leather. The streets were full of un- buried corpses, so that when at last the Spaniards entered the city they tied handkerchiefs over their faces to keep away the stench of rotting flesh.

The resistance had been heroic, but the result was a foregone conclusion. The real struggle, however, was not between two armies but between two civilizations, Indian and European, each of which had its own culture and traditions. This was something which the Mexicans, both Aztecs and those who fought alongside the Spaniards, did not realize until it was too late.

The Mexicans believed that it was a political war on the old tribal pattern, with prizes that could be measured in terms of tribute, power, and prestige. The Spaniards, on the other hand, were fighting a different and more total kind of war. Over and over again they violated the traditional Indian code of chivalry. They attacked without the usual parleying, they killed the enemy instead of trying to take him alive for sacrifice, and, above all, their objectives were different. In Mexican warfare the losers kept their gods, their customs, and, to a large extent, their personal freedom. The aim of the Spaniards, however, was not merely to replace the Aztecs as the ruling power in Mexico, but also to impose a new and alien way of life on a subject population.

For the Aztecs, defeat meant not just a change of allegiance and an increase in taxation, but the end of everything their civilization stood for. In spite of the efforts of a few high-minded clerics and administrators, the Indians lost their cultural identity. Public lands were given to the Spaniards as personal estates, many of the free commoners became serfs, Spanish law replaced Indian law, and the old values no longer had any meaning in the new society. Even the gods were swept aside, and an anonymous Nahuatl poet, writing just after the Conquest, has expressed the bitterness and bewilderment of a people whose gods had deserted them and whose days of glory had suddenly come to an end:

> There is nothing but grief and suffering
> in Mexico and Tlatelolco,
> where once we saw beauty and valour.
> Have you grown weary of your servants?
> Are you angry with your servants,
> O Giver of Life?

Index

The numerals in **heavy type** refer to the figure numbers of the illustrations